Talonbooks • Vancouver • 1992

published with the assistance of The Canada Council

Talonbooks
201/1019 East Cordova
Vancouver, British Columbia
Canada, V6A 1M8

Typeset in Baskerville by Pièce de Résistance Ltée. Printed and bound in Canada by Hignell Printing Ltd.

Second Printing: September 1993,

sum uv thees pomes have previouslee apeerd in prism
intrnashunal sound poetree issew   rampike   quarry   cum
ths way (oxford eng paula claire prod)   cold drill   liquid
wayze (cassett with adeena karasick) jw curry book HOWARD
XPERIENCES   canadian forum   LUDDITES cassett   dreemin uv
th nite   (with gerry collins n murray favro)   cabaret vert
next exit   this cannot b tollorated (st paul minn)   london
life (with chris meloche   nightwood edishyuns)   prism intr
nashyunal langwage issew   mental radio   robert lax & othr
konkreet poets   art galleree buffalo u (travelling) canadian
Literatur

for Evelyn Li

othr animals toys   titul   by   Ben Kennedy

trial uv th selby hotel   writtn with   Ben Kennedy

addenda 2   "   "   writtn with   Joy Kuropatwa

deth by a salesman   titul by   Deborah Oliver

front & back covr photographee   by   Allan Rosen
front covr design by Allan Rosen
back covr design by Karl Siegler

thanks 2 th ontario arts council writrs reserv fund
& th canada council short term project grant 1990

thanks 2 Wendy Wood & George Siu for art show at
Not Just Deserts 1638 east broadway vancouver b.c.

Canadian Cataloguing in Publication Data

Bissett, Bill, 1939 -
inkorrect thots

Poems.
ISBN 0-88922-303-3

I. Title.
PS8503.17815 1992   C811'.54   C92-091200-1
PR9199.3.B5715 1992

bbbbb
RRRRR
eeeee
ttt tt tt
hhh hhh
iii iiiiii
nnnnnn
gg ggg

wer yu falling down

refugee   from th jade town
th winds uv knives n such
uncertaintee   running thru
yr bones

as if ther cud b a lasting home
for yr gestur   isint it in
th beet   meeting th tempo
thats wun way

anothr is my hugging yu
taking yu into th side uv
th mountain   wher i waitid
for yu   my arms bracing yr
fall

ths is diffrent thn whn
i dont beleev

inkorrect thots

WARNING   each wun uv thees
pomes may contain inkorrect
thots   thees pomes have not
bin kleerd by th ministree
uv korrect thots

ths book contains reel storees
that have reelee happend   th
mysteree uv pain has not bin
adequatelee xplaind 2 us   why
memorees can cum crashing down
on us robbing us uv our present
or why we lifting grasp hold uv
a suddn laffing idea   baloons
us up   n what we lern from memorees

i cum skraping across a glacier
bringing yu ths burnd flowr   see
its petals bleed as it opns   all
ovr our plans   our mesurd safetees
see its tabula filling with such
wondrous snow

falling   falling   on th beautiful
wounds   th uncared for moaning in
allees   undr cardbord   whil othrs
walk by   going 2 sumwher   not
stopping   a tree is a tent   us   a
molecule   longing is   i think
recentlee deleetid from consciousness

ther ar an infinitee uv thots being
xpressd heer   ths is langwage   nd an
infinitee uv thots not being xpressd
heer   ther is silens   ther is yr mind
is it   th ministree has not prepard
us for evreething   what is not being
xpressd heer   may b inkorrectlee not
being xpressd   not being xpressd so
inkorrectlee   as 2 hous an infinitee

uv words   ther is no control ovr
what is not being xpressd

ths hous is on th moov   ther have bin
apolojees bfor   they have alredee bin
made   for th peopul who ar not heer
we apologize agen   ther ar word games

signifying much word ecstasee   within
th langwage   n its momenta resembla   a
word uv cawsyun   its own music   sumtimes
inkorrect thots may b byond our control
each wun uv thees pomes may contain an
inkorrect thot

thees pomes have not bin bleerd by
th ministree uv korrect thots   we have
no control ovr what is not being xpressd
heer eithr

byond ths sign   yr on yr own

i was dewing a reeding

in a hi school   n th
toxik land fill   recentlee
discoverd undr th playground
n monitord constantlee was
above what they calld
normal that day

so all th windows uv th
school wer kept closd   th
principal   he sd 2 me   its
bettr 2 b safe than sorree

i certainlee cudint agree
mor i sd   yes   n i recalld
that th universitee had tried
2 fire th left wing professor
who had discoverd th toxik
land fills leeking

in so manee local reel estate
deel sites   so important   2
th ekonomik development uv th
whol communitee

its also terrifik 2 know
what th normal rate uv toxik
leeking is   n

that ther is a normal rate
wun that cant
hurt us

at all   n that just closing
windows can so effektivlee
deel with anee possibul
dangr

n totalee seel off

a building

so much writing is

th presentaysyun uv
conclusyuns tieing up
into portabul bunduls
th dreems ecstasees
n failurs uv our lives
2 let them go relees
them so we can keep
on going

what if we presentid
th non sentimental
non voyaging sceens
that sumtimes haunt us
like our domestik fites
bfor they ar resolvd
if they ar

like I DONT WANT
2 LIVE WITH YU ANEE
MOR GREAT IUL BREK
ALL YR TOYS 2

forgetting in thos times
undr th pressurs uv church
n state n wanting changes
we cant make

th times we made reelee
love with each othr th
promises seeing all th
colors uv th magik birds
lifting us

at first meeting

othr animals toys

i was givn a job kleening a cabin   up in northern
bc   that had bin totalee livd in by a lot uv pack
rats   from th amount uv brokn dishes   rat shit   n
blood   on th floor   i think ther had bin major
parteeing   rats i sd   whn i got th first whiff uv
th smell

n thees huge nests they built   coupul feet hi   n
decoratid with sequins   n brite tiny stones they
had takn off toy animals that had bin in th cabin
bfor they got ther

i kleend an entire day   non stop   scrubbd   carreed
hevee nests out 2 th garbage far away   hammerd thik
metal ovr all th holes that th pack rats had sawd
thru 2 get inside   they had gnawd a hole thru th
front door   evree time i wud slop anothr bucket uv
hot watr n solvent on th floors   i wud hope ths
wud dew it   kleen it   th blood n shit   th smell
scrub   scrub   slop   slop

in wun uv theyr nests   layerd so beautifulee   sequins
shining   brite green grass   i lookd in   THER WAS A
TOY MOUS   that had nevr bin ther bfor   in th cabin
IT WAS THEYRS   TH PACK RATS HAD BROUT THEYR OWN TOY
MOUS INTO TH CABIN   WITH THEM

i now knew that probablee most creaturs on ths planet
love   n have toys   n xperiens speshul delite in
miniturizing   portabul   magik essenses   remindrs

n i knew fr sure th pack rats had brout ths toy mous
with them   i had nevr seen it bfor   tiny n silvree
n hopeful looking

that nite   i was almost asleep   undr th blankit   i
herd a nois   sat up   n saw a huge pack rat staring at
me   i sd   get BACK   i closd all yr doors   YU CUDINT
HAVE GOT IN HEER   i was veree loud

th pack rat noddid   n split back outside

th voices in th blu wallpapr

its a luminous blu with littul
branches n berrees red dots
like tiny strawberrees th voices
i gess climb out on 2 talk they

sd bill yul b getting a nu mind
in ten months i was tuckd in bed
almost asleep o great i sd will
i still share frendships with th
same peopul yes bill yu will they
sd will i still write n paint yes
bill yu will great i sd ium
veree xcitid whn i askd

in ten months th voices in th blu wall
papr repeetid my math can b shakee
so i was counting on my fingrs ten
from late septembr came up with may
i realize now that itul b late july
erlee august thats 1991 ium veree
xcitid looking forward 2 it they addid
that whol seksyuns uv th mind i have now
will start 2 crumbul drop away its so
great 2 make room for th nu mind i think
i can feel th crumbuling starting

coupul nites latr i was in bed goin 2
sleep agen whn th voices in th blu wall
papr surfasing from theyr infinit lumin
ositee sd bill yes i sd n they sd for
yu prsonal happeeness is just around th
cornr i was veree xcitid got out uv bed
my clothes on went out walkd around th
cornr past th prins albert dinr it was
closd it was aftr 4 in th morning

n i felt prsonal happeeness sweep into me
its bin with me evr sins n i went back home
into bed veree happee prsonalee n sd
thanks a lot 2 th wall

unmatching phenomena

a lot uv life is unaccountabul
n can b hard 2 describe   yu
almost have 2 b ther   she was
telling me that her boy frend for
17 yeers was abt 2 die

in penatanguishing prison   he had
killd 7 - 8 peopul   n was a psycho
path   he was diagnosd as that   n
now   he has lung cancr n onlee
a few months 2 live

she had askd him 2 consent 2 being
moovd 2 wellsley st hospital in toronto
rathr than so far away   so they cud
have sum decent conversaysyun for a
whil she sd   he refusd 2 satisfy her on
ths   for 17 yeers she had gone up 2 see
him   at leest 2 times a month   n she
is poor

she told me he wants 2 b with his mothr
in hevn   they had had a terribul relaysyunship
n wants 2 b reunitid with her   n dusint want
th bothr uv mooving whil hes in so much
pain   she begs him n he refuses

in a way ths was his last verbal abuse
uv her she sz

tho as she told me he may have killd 7 - 8
peopul   n she dusint like 2 think abt
that   but she had made manee enquirees
n he had nevr had othr women on th side
had in fact   onlee killd on th side   so
she sd   she had bin luckee

have yu bin singul all ths time i askd
no she sd   i did get marreed for a whil
but ther was nevr th passyun ther   no wun
bfor or sins   no wun like him

what amazd th cab drivr

was nothing had happend
nothing had bin sd   no
misundrstanding   no
aneething   no motiv
no linear aneething 2
leed up 2

th passengr leeping out
uv th back seet   pushing
him undr th steering
wheel   n beeting th shit
out uv him   breking 2
ribs   busting his jaw
knoking three teeth out

th passengr split aftr
that   n th cab drivr pulld
him self togethr   n drove
2 th hospital   wher he
stayd for three daze

he cudint tell them
aneething ther   bcoz
nothing had happend
xcept th beeting   th
passengr had pd th
fare

listn he told me   it
was anothr nite in
london   anothr nite
on erth

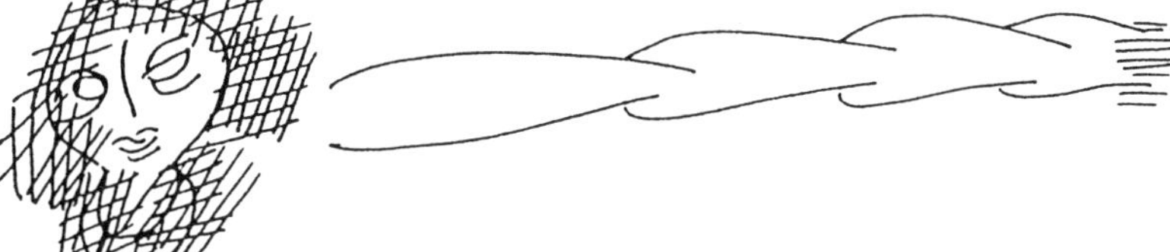

last nite i had a nitemare abt free trade

it was terribul th amrikan govt tuk all our
natchural resources for almost nothing n had
them processd n manufacturd into othr stuff
fr almost nothing in mexico wch also had uh
willinglee enterd into free trade with th
pentagon
we canadians didint have 2 work
anee longr wch was a benefit long snow
dreems in th wintr uninterruptid by anee
thing n summr at th totalee pollutid
beaches cud b relaxing
ther was no munee tho
for curing th increesing
pollusyun n diseeses

amrikan govrnment
helicoptrs kept ruining
our sleep
flying in at all hours

n taking evreething out

soon ther wer no trees
no gud watr
th iron n nickel n sulphur n coal

n hydro powr wer all gone

we had nothing
2 eet

n we still cudint get 2 th far south out uv th
cold canadian wintr fr a whil unless we wer th prime ministr
who was protectid by amrikan c i a soldyeers at all times
from th increesing liklihood uv assasinaysyun
they cudint find aneewun els as co operativ as him not
that ther was aneething els 2 get politikul calmness
tho seemd advisabul n veree canadian
WHAT A

NITE MARE

th inevitabilitee uv tossd salads dictating plesur

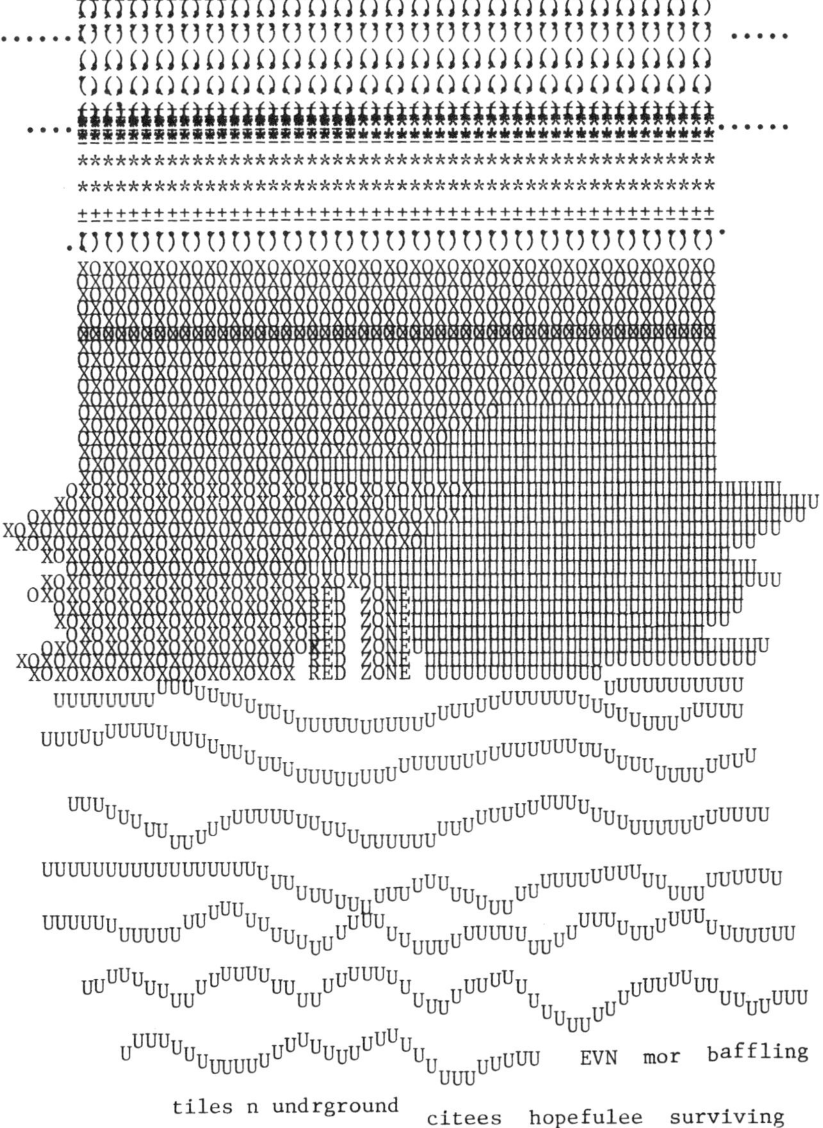
RED ZONE
EVN mor baffling
tiles n undrground citees hopefulee surviving

howard xperiences

i was phoning arleen   n maria answerd   aftr i sd hi
maria sd   HOWARD   how great 2 heer yu   whn ar yu going
2 cum ovr n put a bodee 2 yr vois   how ar yu   ium fine
i sd   how ar yu   she sd it was great 2 heer me   i sd
it was great 2 heer her   thn she sd sum othr xcellent
things   thn ther was a paus   silens   n i sd   is arleen
ther   maria sd howard yu dont evn know arleen   arleen
maria sd   howard wants 2 talk 2 yu arleen   arleen came
2 th phone n sd howard i dont evn know yu   why arint
yu talking with maria   i sd ths isint howard   ths is
bill   its bill arleen sd   maria ths is bill

i was going into th art galleree at 80 spadina   highr
floor   wundrful grittee metal sculptur ther   winding
n fibrous   i was putting up postrs   giving them out   in
vitaysyuns for th opning uv my upcumming art show at th
selby hotel in toronto   n th curator managr i gess uv
ths galleree cum up 2 me as i was entring n askd   what
is th message   walking tord me   was i an oracul   dont
we oftn forget who we ar n think we cud b what sumwun
els thinks we ar   th message is evreebodee i sd   kinduv
takn aback   n reelee feeling i bettr cum up with sumthing
heer   what companee ar yu with he furthr enquird   mor
insistent   ium with th companee uv evreebodee   we had
now reechd as far as we cud in our misplacd xpektaysyuns
uv each othr   i driftid off 2 chek into th sculpturs
he was ovr by his desk   scratching his hed   thn a guy
in a message courrier uniform came in   gave him th
message   n left   thn th curator came ovr 2 me n sd ium
sorree   now i was scratching my hed   whn i left i sd
2 him   i hopd iud see him at th opning   n gave him sum
postrs n invite cards   n he agen sd ium sorree   n agen
i sd   i dont know why   thats okay

i was cumming back 2 london aftr th opning at th selby
it was a beautiful opning   evreewun was great   i was
reelee happee   it had gone so well   lot uv work went into
it   or play   if we revers th meening   n dont we want 2   n
th hotel was great   th train was pulling out uv th
staysyun   ths prson   he was talking abt we cud have wun
free beverage   how much mor wud b n what 2 dew if n what
he cud dew 2 make th trip mor comfortaybul for us   he was
xcellent   via at its finest fr sure   most peopul wer al

redee sleeping or into theyr audio music machines i felt sad for him dewing all that talking it was well ovr 5 minits no wun reelee looking at him or listning it was his job 2 say th whol thing thn he sd sumthing i tuk 2 b was ths all cleer did we all undrstand totalee he was quite a wayze away from wher i was sitting he was at th othr end uv th train ther was a lot uv train nois i was tirud i made th sign for positivitee with my fingrs 2 reassur him he had i latr gessd askd if thr was aneewun who spoke french onlee he tuk my sign 2 indicate that he came ovr stood next 2 me n repeetid th whol thing all ovr 5 minits uv it en français he was veree great i lookd at him veree appresiativlee thruout his whol talk whn he was thru i sd merci he was veree happee so was i

whn sumwun sz yr name

i melt n float inside
th centr uv my chest wher

th reel heart is singing

thn at nite i entr th
doubting castul n

ache

i usd 2 see them walking cross th train

tracks him always weering a reelee old beet up
swetr i remembr it as dirtee beize tho it cud also
have bin green n veree rumpuld ther cud have bin
two swetrs he wud weer n smoking constantlee n she
on his arm talking so animatidlee n close walking
just ahed uv a strong lake breez lukilee curing th
humiditee blu sky yello sun wun uv th best daze
that can happn in london ontario beautiful

i wud say hi 2 them n them 2 me it was cool a
flash uv recognishyun xchangd iud seen him a lot on
local tv heer in london wher he held a talk show
counselling peopul giving advice n support 2 peopul
with various addicksyuns

he was veree helpful 2 othr peopul

thn nowun saw him for what seemd 2 long

he didint answr his phone neithr did she howevr th
wethr was

it rang n rang

thn it was th smell th terribul smell that finalee
attracktid neighbours 2 his apartment

n whn th police arrivd n enterd they found her
knawing eeting wun uv his arms he had bin uv
cours ded for weeks

they cudint charge her with cannibalism that was no
longr on th books in canada

she had beetn him 2 deth was it impropr care uv
human remains

was it unsanitaree condishyuns was it culinaree
indesensee

certainlee sum disagreement was thot 2 have occurrd

yu know what scientists have bin dewing with canarees

recentlee they have bin observing canarees n finding
that boy canarees have song boxes in theyr brains they
line up on tiny logs n sing for th girl canarees who
select th boy canarees with th song they like best girl
canarees dont have thees song boxes

ths frcckd out contemporaree scientists they had decidid
that ther wer no gendr diffrences that wer at all a big
deel independent uv th effects uv condishyuning

so th doktors painlesslee enterd th girl canarees brain
th artikul in discoveree magazeen emphasizd th word pain
less n agen painlesslee tickuld th girl canarees brain
n she bgan singing having herself now grown a song box
from th tickuling n she was lining up 2 sing for th boy
canarees who wer thn selecting th song bird they liked
th best

i was givn ths magazeen by th guy next 2 me in th bus going
south thru th fraysyr canyun bcoz i was having ths painless
olfactoree hallusinaysyun evree thing was chocolate th
huge smells uv chocolate oozing thruout th bus totalee
iuv had kaka olfactoree hallusinaysyuns bettr th chocolate
thn th kaka probablee from travelling fateeg th guy next
2 me suggestid th discoveree magazeen mite help 2 reed what
theyr dewing with birds

theyr finding out that birds use all uv theyr brain n that
they voluntarilee migrate wheras in school i had bin taut
that birds onlee involuntarilee migrate yes birds send
scouts ahed 2 chek out th wethr patterns is it cool 2 fly
ther they make all kinds uv great willd decisyuns n heers
th big part they use all uv theyr brains n whn a synapse
pops or a neuron burns birds have an enzyme that grows
anothr wun immediatelee we on th othr hand use onlee 1O
pr cent uv our brain tho last nite on tv it sd we use
onlee 4 pr cent its dropping fast hurree so if sumwun
calls me bird brain agen i know its a wundrful complement
n can say thanks

what ar we saving our unusd porsyun uv our brain for
th othr 90-96 pr cent   in such fallow   is it in case uv
sum emergensee   sumthing veree serious cumming up   we
know chocolate opns th same parts uv th brain as duz
falling in love   we know chocolate adds watr 2 th brain
birds use all uv theyr brain n regrow neurons all th time
we dont dew eithr uv thos   why not   what ar we waiting
for   can we b painlesslee tickuld   n by who

if we can xtract th enzymes   from th birds brains   pain
lesslee uv cours n duplikate it   n inject it into ours
we cud heel ourselvs   brain damage   brain stem injurees
so much   maybe alzheimers   its encouraging 2 think uv

our politishyans fly a lot   th mulroonee govrnments flite
bills ar in th millyuns   why arint they using all uv theyr
brains   why arint they singing   logik is not th onlee
driving fors in th univers

iuv bin secreetlee thinking   prhaps we ar saving th rest
uv th brain for sum reelee big ocasyuns   like th meeting
uv minds   whn th visitors reveel themselvs   n we all join
hands   alredee tickuld   n singing   ocasyuns   that so far
havint happend

evn if birds dont watch tv   or watr flowrs   write pomes
build bridges   or have marital arguments   ar they anee
less than us   gulls uv cours terrorize puffins   ripping
theyr eggs apart   flying off with yolk hanging   out uv theyr
beeks   thats part uv th othr side uv bird life   its hard
2 know what 2 idealize

like th time a literaree frend sd 2 me   at th beginning uv
a poetree gathring   that so n so wudint b heer for ths nites
reedings   that he cud onlee cum on saturdaze

no i sd   thats terribul

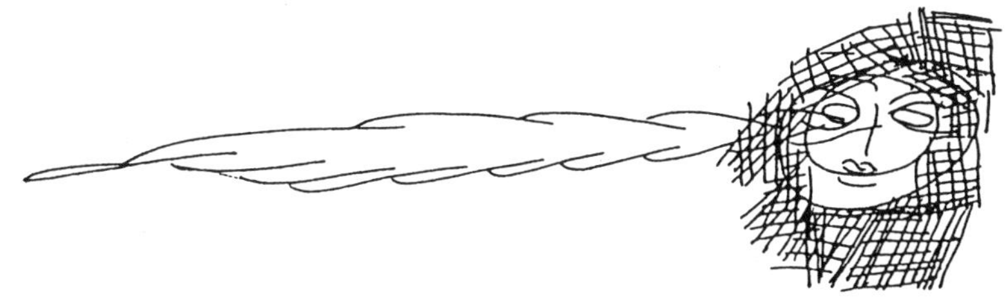

th lime woolvs outside lightning creek touching in side

our hearts beeting isint ther sumthing els we cud get
into i sd 2 him mooving closr into his enerjee standing
ther ths turquois lake its all getting coldr snow n bits
uv ice apeering darting in th lips uv th watr moovd by
th lime gleem from th woolvs eyez ar staring at us th
lake th biggest moon uv th yeer i sd as he put his hands
btween my legs closing in on me taking my buttons off my
chest picking at th nippuls me breething him with
each stroke his hands across my peks guiding me down
kneeling btween his spreding legs inside th covring uv ths
willo breething stretching so far from being anee cold
th lime woolvs not mooving looking out at us th now calm
agen watrs glazd fire our loving moovments all th voices
invisibul fethrs singing peopul voices choruses rush
thru th treez branches stirring memorees leevs passyun
evreething lives burning evreething run on storees in th
frakshurd ice air stinging rush tord us th lake spins
on in our eyez startuls rattuls in ours th woolvs eyez
glowing i feel his tongue in my spine bellee chest ium
turning on ths moon lake his fur my tongue in him so
mooving in me us both turning in th woolvs nevr moov
ing closr theyr holding toed on a snowee ledg ten
metrs away in ths wind cumming up we all smell each othr
in my spine bellee chest ium turning on his fingrs ar
holding my nippuls rubbing ar gathring bunching my chest
my neck shouldrs starting 2 sing bcum sensual agen th
work load soshul bag dropping from me th reel dreem
returning continuing th othr side wher th plesur is
being togethr th woolvs burning lime colord eyez
th branches uv th willo its closing around us wer
bathing in th lime rays melon tropikul etchd lite
in th 30 below ice turquois watrs lites in th air
ice sky breth snow falling is falling our eye lids
mouths almost 2 talk catch ice on th sylabuls breeth
ing togethr us like sum time goez on forevr our
lime eyez burning knowing all ways all ways n ths
way carrees us home

th fevr peopul

aftr assuring all
theyr frends   on th phone
that theyul not go out n will stay
inside   theyr blankits   n take theyr
pills   n try 2 keep theyr
fevr down   will   wuns nowun mor
will call   or if thers no wun mor 2
call   will get theyr clothes back on
n sneek out n rage with an
atlantik tossing romanticism
edgar alan poe   in th driving rain
or whatevr   n feel xcellent for
an hour   strangrs passing saying
yu look so gud
thn th limbs tirud uv
plodding   plodding   feel suddnlee   like
collapsing   find theyr way home   n
fall sweting in th bed
wondr
abt life   n romanticism   n
sentimentalitee   th long journees
we take 2 b with sum wun we love
n so cleerlee undrstand th psychik
necessitees uv theyr own life
like broadcast news   th xplanaysyuns
keep cumming   speeding byond
comprehensyun
STOP yr going
2 fast

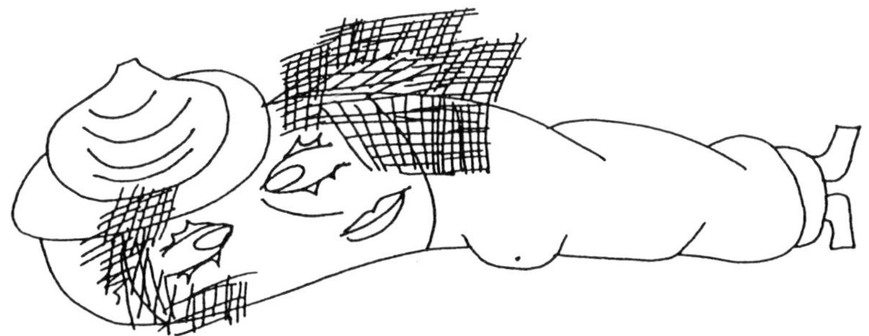

rivr running thru th erth 2 th see

....
....
.... think we cud control th time uv th tides ....
.... think we cud change th rush uv th ocean ....
XXXXXXX now that yr ther n i am heer XXXXXXXXXX
XXXXXXX now that yr ther n i am heer XXXXXXXXXX
XXXXX th gourd in my hed turns me shakes me XXX
XXXXX th gourd in my hed turns me shakes me XXX
our hands ar touching in th mooving subway XXXXX
XXXXX ium getting XXXXXXXXXXXXXXXXXXXXXXXXXXXX
th word
.... deliveree ....
.... we find our own ways 2 th see we find our ....
own ways 2
th see

.... think we cud control th time uv th tides ....
.... think we cud change th rush uv th ocean ....
XXXXXX now that yr ther n i am heer XXXXXXXXX
XXXXXXX now that yr thr n i am heer XXXXXXXXX
XXXXXX th gourd in my hed turns me shakes me
XXXXXX th gourd in my hed turns me shakes me
our hands ar touching in th mooving subway
XXXXX ium getting XXXXXXXXXXXXXXXXXXXXXXXXXXXXXXXX
no wun like yu 2 (th word) wash away th care
XXXXXXXXXXXXXXXXXXXXXXXXXXXX deliveree XXXXXXXXX
no wun like yu for me X XXXXXXXXX
we find our own ways 2 th see we find our
own ways 2
th see
we find our own ways 2 th see
we find our
own ways 2
th see
....
2 th see 2 th see 2 th see 2 th see 2 th
2 th see 2 th see 2 th see 2 th see 2 th
2 th see 2 th see 2 th see 2 th see 2 th
2 th see 2 th see 2 th see 2 th see 2 th
2 th see 2 th see 2 th see 2 th see 2 th
2 th see 2 th see 2 th see 2 th see 2 th
....
....
....

maydee

wun morning in th prins albert dinr paul
was complaining abt how tirud he was n
j d came in n sd he was xhaustid with life
n th various pursuits othr peopul within
wer groaning abt diffrent parts uv theyr
bodeez not getting anee satisfacksyun or
had 2 much xistenshul pain abt theyr lives
n limbs

i sd mistr paul yu ar 2 young for tirudness
like that arint yu n j d dont b in pain
yet ther cud b mor 2 cum for all uv us
theyr all looking at me blanklee n saying
like okay bill thn maydee sitting next 2
me sd ium 83 ium not tirud just got back
from a caribbean cruis th tiny bubbuls
circuit n ths man askd me 2 marree him
but hes 92 n i think hes 2 old for me duz
age mattr i askd she sd in ths case it cud
in th romanse department hes a reel lust
macheen but in his hed hes old fashyund
sins ium th woman he wants me 2 cook n kleen
i dont know what 2 dew she sd whats he
offring i askd

a condo in florida maydee answerd how manee
bed rooms i askd as manee as i want she sd
well get 3 or 4 i sd n iul cook n kleen
th guys in th band cin stay ther as well n
we can dew gigs ther just tell him yu cookd
th dinnrs n also yu cud tell him that we ar
temporaree visitors iul think abt that she
sd

n as she was leeving she sd theyr still
complaining abt aches n pains yu just got 2
rock on n she ragd out

next day maydee at th countr i sit next 2
her ask her whats th latest she sd i turnd
him down i hate a man who begs o i sd

so she sd thers anothr guy heer in town n
he loves me but hes 67 hes 2 young i dont think
age is that important i sd she sd i think ium
going 2 get out uv my building why i askd she
sd theyr all old ther n they koff all th time
n theyr not smoking she tuk in sum mor black
coffee n anothr puff uv her cigarett i dont
koff she sz mistr paul sz we all dew well
maydee sd i was born way bfor pollusyun so my
lungs have had manee unpollutid yeers that
makes a big diffrens

most peopul in th dinr wer still hanging theyr
heds abt life isint it an almost universal mode
we sumtimes go for i notisd she held her hed up
she showd me picturs uv her n th man she turnd
down dansing happee all nite long she sd she
pickd up her purs shed finishd her coffee her
purs matchd all her clothes today it was cherree
shirt jacket skirt coat hat white trim shes
beautiful walking out so strong thru th white snow
n th 20 below see yu soon bill she had sd

next day we had coffee she sd she wud like 2 see
her mothr soon shes getting on maydee sd we dont
live forevr she sd we want 2 keep up th kontacts
how old is she i askd 110 she sd she sd th man
heer in town is 2 dependent on her n thats no gud
she had bin marreed 58 yeers had bin happee n
didint want 2 get in a mess now i want 2 love a
man she sd not get screwd up reelee i sd

whn she left we sd 2 each othr lets start feeling
bettr

i wondrd wher maydee was n i had bin out uv town
coupul uv daze went in 2 th dinr n she was at th
countr sat next 2 her th wethr was improoving n
so wer all our moods she sd 2 me bill ium going
on anothr cruis shed onlee bin back coupul weeks
wher 2 i askd th caribbean agen she sd with 3
women no men she sd

i hope yu have a wundrful time i sd i will she sd

yu know bill th onlee thing that bothrs me sum time is that i think my husband lovd me way mor than i lovd him n her tendr eyez teering whil she sd ths i dont think he evr knew i sd or he wud have sd sumthing dun sumthing abt it n if he lovd yu so much it made up for that xtra lacking he didint care he lovd yu so much n i think yu did love him as much as he lovd yu yu miss him terriblee n yu ar veree brave try not 2 have regrets i know i sd evree day i deel with diffrent small n large regrets n evree day i let go uv them stay in th present living from ther sum daze thats easier than othrs it can b dun tho on a dailee basis yes bill i think thats it what u sd ium looking for sum thing 2 b sad abt whn i dont reelee need 2 x cept 2 watr my eyes a bit they have bin getting 2 dry i want 2 b happee sumtimes life is getting yr face on n going out thats th first step but wer still breething arint we she sd 2 me yes i sd we ar

she was getting up 2 go iul take care uv th coffee i sd thank yu bill see yu soon have a wundrful time i sd 2 her i will bill i will yu know she sd yu just got 2 rock on yu know she sd 2 me i know i sd i know

dragons in th sky

for Deborah Oliver

sumtimes we soar so hi
sumtimes we swoop so low
sumtimes our dreems go on forevr
but cummin home yu
know we ar veree close
2 th ground aftr all

watchin th dragons in th sky moov
watchin th dragons in th sky change
watching th dragons in th sky danse
watchin th dragons in th sky go

th moon turns us in th soil
th fire burns us in th wheel
th bones n heart mend cure
n start agen

watchin th dragons in th sky moov
watchin th dragons in th sky change
watching th dragons in th sky danse
watchin th dragons in th sky go

we listn 2 th magik voices
heeling our mind th loons
n th sky call out thru th
fetheree air
n th nite is softr n softr softr
n softr still
n mor ther
wher we ar
closr 2 th ground

watchin th dragons in th sky moov
watchin th dragons in th sky change
watching th dragons in th sky danse
watchin th dragons in th sky go

each nite aftr septembr

i lay puttin yr spells on me
n th heart n flesh rising agen yu know no wun cums thru
th door
in ths dimensyun our pants n shirts off n th

clock is ticking so n th nervs evn embrace yu n
th telling gesturs i nevr
forget tho i forgot yu wudint b
heer in ths world
eye came 2
who can change th road
fast enuff for aneething th leevs whirling n dropping
like antlrs thud hard on th freezing ground i nevr shuddr
with th crashing treez th falling buildings eye can watch
othrs finding th agilitee uv theyr loving as i have so oftn
in ths spheer
a thousand kilometers away
or staring
off into space so nervus that th qwestyun didint
reelee
reech me feel enclosd in sum wun elsus mind plans
for my proteksyun like wher wud ths take me iul b still
around i say dejectud yu walk off into th cars peopuld
with wishes wishing or i just didint want yu
if th target is th heart or th
loving uv each part uv th
bodee ium off so much th mark
n waiting til each day goez
in ths first frost

n what ium feeling no words for smell th sage th longing
is so giving letting th mercuree flow it is a strange vial
resplendent with tracings engravings uv treez leevs
stark n lush both approaches 2
line n succumbing
streeming up 2 th skies
n th dragon clouds craydul th
steeming moon ovr th

offis towrs

in anothr dimensyun

listning 2 countree n cooking th kitchn in th 4 bar
patterns iuv vacuumd n dun a lot uv papr play n sum
painting n writing n talking on th phone

thru th wires all
our voices carree thees veree intricate n codified messages

its likc singing so manee flowrs still above th ground

or get it on n it is what it is

th island is rocking in th dreem uv th turquois see

th ring encasd in th silvr protects yu from th missing

memorees n trusting th

possibul love heer in ths

town rolling into wintr th great lakes n sky sumtimes

shaking th erth

eye dreemd wun uv my glasses fell out i
dreem oftn ium back with yu thats mor a wish than a dreem

rocking in th changing n lines like aftr getting it on

with yu i dont want 2 cruis no mor apeer n othr

lines uv th coastal area
in ths song

drinking th cup uv my dreems i didint kno iud miss yu at all

or ths much n th road is can i qwestyun it aneething rolling
anothr wun
or up 2 put it 2 mor than it can hold ium

taking it all in with yr arms around me n yu sd th

painting is singing now
our legs rising our mouths
opning 2 th streeming liquids
our spines bcum can
anee wun change th road
willowee touch th ivoree

boats n elephants seeking sheltrs in th lost

forest we look for

we heer th crying

n th husk uv our

milkee need th futur

thats anothr song

or storee

in london ontario

john street is onlee
2 blocks long

theyr not telling th
whol storee

from th amount a
johns in london

i think john street
cud b a whol lot

longr

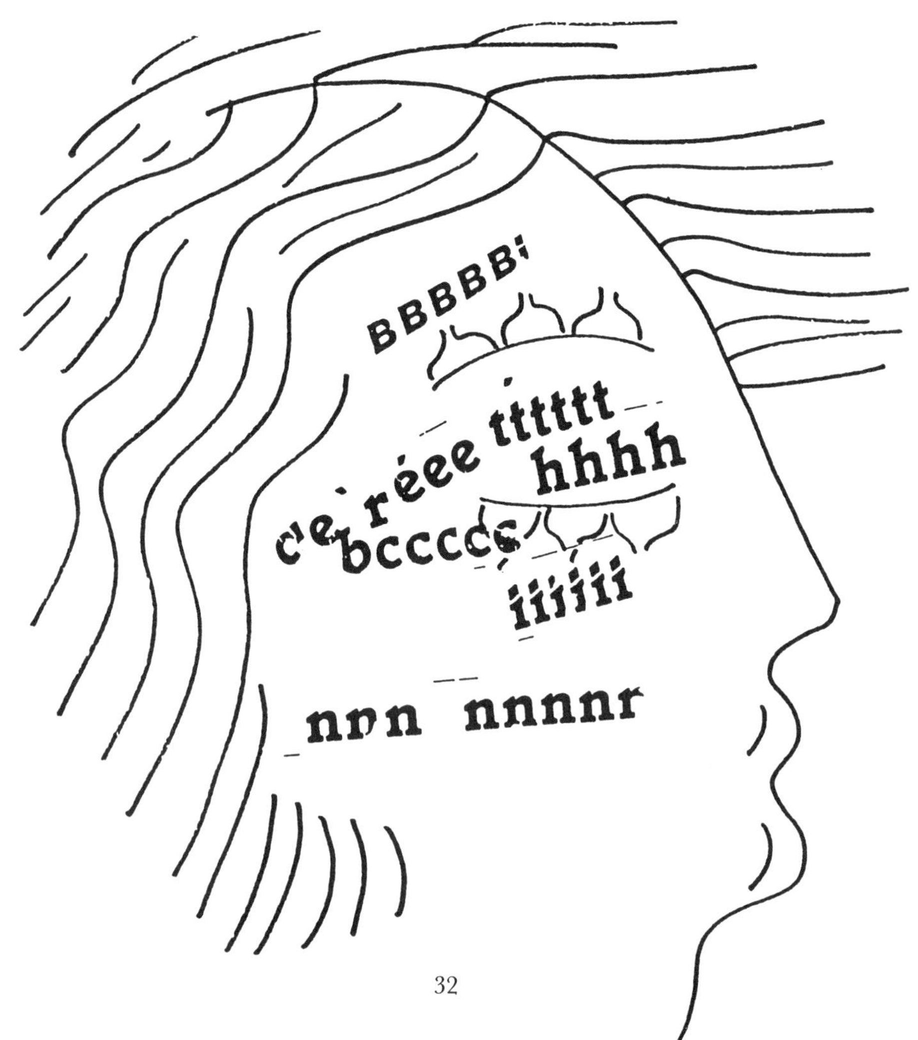

go on serching serching still am

tho i forget it sum now n live in th
words n images fall asleep evn happilee
love how th crows n ravens fill th room
in th morning fleshing out th air

th ideel nothing is lightning flashes
we run on in th sky asking finding

whn yu wake up in th morning wondring wher
ar th crows n ravens filling th room
they wer heer ystrday now i see them

evn having bin ther heer in thees branches
ths hand like yrs serching serching

has lovd so manee

for beautee

we will lay down our arms
our intelligens our resund
planning our wars

n thn we want 2 keep it n
we pick up our arms our
confusyuns our generals
our wars n blow it

2 bits a prfect chin a
wundrful skin tone in
th darkness breething
rising 2 heet an eyebrow
n a leg shifts inviting

a mouth so ripe for

kissing

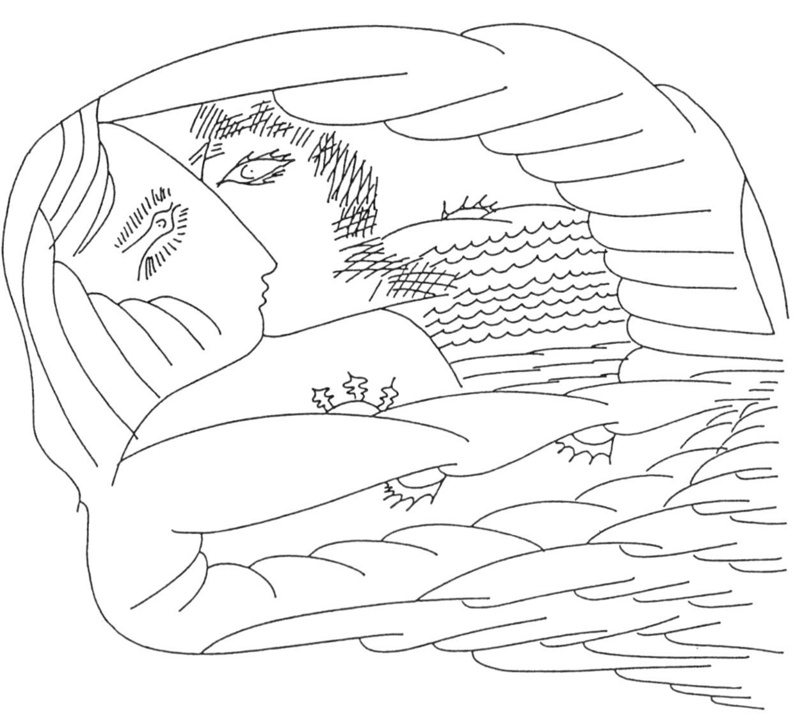

mor inkorrect thots

smugguld out uv th compound without authoritee

iuv writtn yu manee times now n th rivr is running
prettee hi 2day   we moov our houses 2 highr ground
all thru th music announsments wer being made intro
versyuns into our own psychee th possibilitees for
freedom wud yu be being back soon or dew yu find it 2
limiting heer   th ceiling in th temporaree group
hous is veree low   we ar not allowd 2 touch   eye dont
know if i will b allowd 2 leev 2 find yu   th educators
keep a close watch at nite   i dreem uv yu   yr arms
around me   they censor evree pees uv writing heer what
i cant say   how wundrful th pees n trust felt btween
each othr soon they say th communitee can b trustid 2
b free   ther is still they say 2 much devians   it needs
2 b erasd n absorbd into th greatr love uv th communitee
n its fine familees   necesitating ths prolongd interim
period or phase   i hope we have a littul smoke n fire 2
not go compleetlee crazee with ths instruksyun they say
it wunt take 2 much longr 2 b happilee ordinaree 2 b
assimilatid into th greatr gud   i dont think iul evr
get th hang uv it   nor dew i want 2 evr   at nite i dreem
uv yr______mooving into my mouth   my heart   i hope ths
lettr gets 2 yu   whn th rivr goez down   if ium not 2 tirud
from th lecturs n bullshit ium going 2 try th rivr 2 get 2
yu   at nite i heer th drum inside me   beeting so loud in
my hed   in th middul uv th nite they wake me n give me
injecksyuns   i dont know what they ar   sumtimes i forget
abt yu   n thn th images cum back 2 me   yr mouth   eyez
ium holding on 2   as thees assholes keep trying 2 make me
theyrs   is ths th place uv bone breking demons   now theyr
hurrahing compleet obedians 2 theyr wills   i know they
ar just childrn looking for a strong leedr   but eye
gotta get outta heer   they also kill peopul   mor n mor
see yu soon   take care   burn ths aftr yuv red it pleez
iul b with yu soon   remembr th olive treez we slept
undr bside th still n running rivr   that was so
much that time   take care   iul b with yu veree
soon i hope

it tuk 80 milyun

yeers 2 develop
ths moment   th line
for th eye   n th
lid n th brow
breething out from
th blank papr ium
drawing on

i sd 2 her as she
brout me   a filet
uv sole n a gingr
ale   ths humiditee
is fritning

she was waitress
in th restaurant
n a frend

we wer laffing
now   whatul we
dew   thats it
she sd adding

sumtimes i feel
like skreeming

i recognizd ths n askd
evn with th ups
n downs n workin
n health ok   n th
plesurs   whn ar
they she sd

we wer both
thinking uv our
selvs n othr peopul

so dew i sumtimes
2 i sd what
she sd

feel like skreeming

we both know ths
has 2 dew with

we need a brek
get fuckd get
luckee whatevr
n we ar luckee

it cud b way wors

n ths humiditee
is veree skaree

it is what it is
septembr fateeg

toronto 2 hot n
so much changing
n not changing n we
dew feel like

skreeming

ths is th paliativ ward th nurs sd

for Stephen Weir

we like 2 have our familee in gud hands   now ths
servis availabul thru a frend uv mine   as it happns
coinsidens   is onlee 3,500.00 n christian prayrs ar
sd   yu dont want th welfare rates uv free   we want
our familee handuld well dont we   n thees othr wuns
also familee   ar gud frends uv mine   theyr 6,000.00
its onlee coinsidens   th nurs went on   we wer both
crying   he was going soon   i had just sd reelee gud
bye 2 him   tho i sd see yu in a bit   n my frend who
wud b with him til he went   n ths prson was selling
us a christian box whil th time she felt was   rite
i sd   forget it   2 her   i wantid 2 say get away from
us   i sd forget it   she went 2 th staff room   with
her calculator   n her christian prayrs   looking calm
n punching numbrs   we wer in th elevator wch was
designd 2 cum 2 onlee that ward   wher whn i was first
ther with my frend 2 see stephen a nurs told me n
michael that not all uv th peopul in ths ward   have
aids   sum ar just veree old   or have cancr   i had
kissd stephen on th forhed   our eyez totalee meeting
he was always so gud 2 me   michael left me for him
but i nevr didint like him for that   or aneething
i always respectid him n came 2 love him

aftr 3 yeers uv chemotherapee   drugs   diets   cancrs
in th mouth   throat   lungs   skin   decreesing n in
creesing   pain   pain   temporaree improovments   relapses
mor   pain   amazing independens   n so well cared for by
michael   n michael nevr left   nowun reelee left aneewun
so great   until now   will stephen b leeving soon   who
can handul ths   he was receeving a constant supply uv
morpheen now   bones n spirit now   n such strong courage
th morpheen was keeping him out uv most uv th pain
most   not all   tho it made his mind foggee he sd   th
doktor sd soon they wud decrees th dose   it was onlee
for ths short whil   ther wasint much els 2 dew xcept 2
say things like that   weul let whats still in th bottul
run its cours   iuv herd thos remarks bfor   i know what
they meen

anothr nurs sd   have a look around   th tv room   th
balconee with th cedar n plants   recentlee she sd
sumwun passd on   with aids   baloons wer releesd into
th sky he cud see whn he tuk his last breth   it was
veree beautiful she sd

michael was with stephen whn they brout him mor oxygen
2 nites aftr i saw him   he sd   no   pushing it away
i dont want anee mor uv that   it was time for him 2
go   n he went   like that   deep in rest   i was home
down town   i phond th hospital   he was going soon   i

cud feel it whn he left heer   erth   ther was a lifting

a rush   n th feeling uv fethrs mooving   space   his

journee   awe   for that time relees   from th pain n

th suffring   freedom from that   forevr   a feeling

uv wondr   n strength   no teers   they came   bfor   n

aftr

alexandr uv metatarsils

th genius uv hop sparrows
brout us irrevocablee into th deepest draft regyun
uv th caverns n outside all evreewher th falling
snow
on our plans
shapes uv huge snow birds
elegantlee n ferventlee holding on to th

trunks as if they wer resting in

such great bliss theyr toe

nails humming into th bark th purpul trees

bathd n coverd in frothee snow
drifts

shapes uv horses shapes uv faeree dominyuns

shapes uv faeree countrees now its time we

stoppd at last snowd in ther is no going

onlee staying its 28 below n th snow drifts as

well on th road totalee closing it for anee

going cumming
hanging icikuls on our dreems

a faeree captain face in th snow trees looking alarmd

whn th powr goes off
will we all make it
n getting
it take it eezee on thees wuns shit yeh we dont

find ourselvs out in it
looking for cake sleepee

licorice
dreems keeping th fire going

all th time

its ourselvs we keep warm dont need
reelee leedrs or promises
ium not lonlee

i paintid th purpul braid

i ran out uv storees i sd n
wantid to write writing thats anothr storee in th middul
th yello shape cud seem to divide th painting into two
tho it dusint all th colors n shapes n enerjees on eithr
side complement each othr enuff that th balansing is main
taind showing a musical tensyun cyclops went on hammring
pointing to th lectern in th paint n shapes n disapeering
reapeering figures an interest continuing n
i saw th forms
agen in th trees frothee wing snow clumps n clustrs
radiant ovr
protektiv uv th sap angels leening ovr th
uprite n yerning fingrs towrs uv th erth

breething
angel birds what els can yu want

all th wanting n gettings its so non minimal n so

baroque
OR all th reesons against adventuring
if its romanse
go for it
n if its too erlee still take
yr time think
sage n yr life is wundrful my frend he

sd to me

n th snow n th sky n th fire n th watr

n th erth undr

th faeree beings xultant in

ths great snow scoot ovr

breething deep in th magik

snow watr crystal fire

changes

byond treetment

so i got 2 th psychiatrist

i wantid help with th why i get sick
so oftn thot that counseling mite
help i thot n he sd i was 2 unstaybul
for help i was 2 crazee for treetment
he cudint help didint he sd have that
kind uv time had i told him 2 much

i was byond treetment   he insistid

i wud get sickr n mor depressd during self
xaminaysyun mite not evr get bettr now at
leest i get bettr frequentlee he sd

he addid that iud obviouslee developd
methods uv coping ths long n he didint
think iud surviv anee tinkering with it
so he sd he cudint take me   kept demanding
my OHIP numbr

so i left feeling a bit i gess rejectid
it was pouring rain iud askd if i cud
use his phone 2 call a cab   he sd he
didint have a phone unbeleevabul so
i walkd home went for a veree long nap
th cockroaches left me alone for a whil
feeling like a pome returnd by a magazeen
sent back not rite for us at ths time
a bit baffuld sum releevd was it wun
less thing 2 worree abt   mor time 2
write n paint   isint that what its abt

n laying ther suspending btween releef
n puzzulment   thers so much 2 say i dont
kno wher 2 finish sumtimes whn th dogs
uv fateeg ar barking at my hed wake up
coverd agen in swet n my face with now
cockroaches crawling ovr theyr zillyun
tiny legs brushing my tite skin ar they

saying ther ther   dont worree leeving
theyr indecipherabul messages on my eyelids

raising th valu on all our gwestyuns   what
we let go uv   is it our luck   2 keep going
we encountr   they thot they werent resisting
they wer   th politeness   no   they lovd   was
it 2 dominate   i lovd   was it 2 pleez   blah
blah   za boo bee   no   ther was loving   sharing
changing   situaysyuns   lern   lern   lern   unlern
wanting so much   2 vacuum

is anee bedroom safe   dew th rich want evreething
dew men reelee like killing as much as they seem
2   what can th soul dew   duz it leev th bodee
as soon as it can

weighs   what   5   7   ounces   is seldom seen   out

at nite   looking   like   life   sum   peopul

feel   it goez   on   2 long

i have nevr forgottn

seeing on tv all th
men uv th conservativ
n liberal partees n
evn sum

uv th ndp tho not all

laffing whn a membr uv
th ndp i think it was

grace mcginnis tried
2 bring in a bill against
wife battring

n all thos men who now
think war is so justified
wer laffing n laffing

n laffing n laffing

i saw ths

its a fact

iul always

remembr it

talk abt yr
bottom lines

talk abt yr
ass holes

each day

bcumming n being frends with
th dictator   was less eezee

always at th close uv a day
howevr simplee spent ther wer
fresh challenges   angr   ordrs
layd at my door   by him

what was his problem

his kindness   so genuin seeming
quikleee replacd   with no
warning   or provokaysyun
by myself   or aneewun   with
sum slamming remark   sum authoritativ
powr drive

th list uv wch 2 numerous   or hed   achee
2 mensyun   at ths time

i thot being frends   with th dictator
wud make him   less controlling   on a
numbr uv okaysyuns

i assurd him that i
i assurd him that i

cared for him   evn tho his
behaviour was eroding my trust
in othrs   n myself

it was not my problem

i came 2 realize   i had livd with th
dictator manee times   had bin his advisor
in mattrs uv pees   th dictator had not
always bin a man

i also thot that   he was making hedway
getting bettr   less controlling   n

me also getting bettr in not being so
dfensiv or afrayd or angree at him his
getting bettr that hadint workd

gradualee his controlling powr trips evn
with me howevr obleeklee speeking up evn
his limitid confessyuns bcame 2 much for me
2 grok was i controlling

i wore thin uv encouraging th dictators mor
human side thinking i was helping him his
isms wer hurting me his manipulaysyuns

i didint need anee
longr i had nevr needid dipping into
roles
slipping into teeching pleez
eesing into being
not anee mor 2 cajole
or encourage or leed
th dictator 2 th
peesful watr
i didint need aneemor th worrees

th dictator thot uv a nu ploy he confessd
his controlling urges

i sd i 2 have tried 2 control n have givn
that up not reelee trew but wanting 2 b sympathetik
offring him comraderee tho also taking his
responsibilitee for his acksyuns away from
him
at last that not working ther was no longr
a role for me reassuring n helping th dictator
bcum mor human evn th wun time i stood up 2
him
or mor than that he sd he was resigning
i acceptid that ths time rathr than helping him anee
mor b bettr n stay on did he go on 2 manipulate
othrs thees yeers had bin enuff for me

th roles etsetera i didint want i wantid 2 b wher
onlee wuns heart cud grow ths giving heart 2 th
dictator wasint working eithr

helping th dictator bcum mor human

that was no longr my hope

it was up 2 him as it had always bin

tho i wasint yet compleetlee in
th cleer

i no longr needid th
dictator

has life alredee startid did i miss much

so usd 2 crises   i was living with ths
guy in a foreign countree   n nothing was
going wrong   n i cud live ther forevr n
evreething was being takn care uv   it was
a big hous   was it big enuff for me
he askd   abt th hous

so much wasint going wrong that it made me
veree nervus   n i was taking valium a lot
i had bin interrogatid for almost three
hours at th bordr   evn tho i thot i lookd
veree strait   heud go 2 sleep n i cudint
tell what i was feeling   or feel his angr
aneemor   what was he angree abt   was it me
ther was nothing going on inside me

i wud take small blus bfor going 2 sleep
at nite   evreething was so calm i cudint draw
or write   it was a kind uv ultima calma
wher no mental activitee   or creativ   activitee
cud take place   i wasint complaining   but thr
was no intracksyun   was i being   old fashyund
so th pills helpd

on my own   n no angr   evn whn he wantid 2 have
his dog with us whn we wud b getting it on   i
didint mind it with his casuala visitori   wun
sighing aftr   heud nevr got it on with a canad
ian bfor   but not with a veree small dog

n he sd he didint think my monkee was reel
thats whn i knew   evn 2 have it all   cud have
a veree hi price   n i missd th prson i usd 2
live with who left me   n heer i was   trying
2 change

he askd me not 2 speek with his aunt   whn we
wer delivring a taybul 2 her   evreewun lookd
at me whn we wer in th park togethr   i liked

aunt a lot n wavd at her aneeway she
liked me i cud tell n wavd back at me
it wasint speeking

sumwher bneeth gravitee ther ar so manee
unresolvd emosyuns n problems with all
ths nevr getting cleer or not

whn i left he sd 2 his dog say gudbye 2
bill hes going back 2 a foreign countree

i wonderd is ths reelee weird enuff

n like life it had startid out so

veree promising

evreewun needs a gud fuck n th rest is bullshit jack sd

i dont know i sd
if onlee th generals n th leedrs uv whatevr wud as he
sd certain what gets in th way uv that whethr self imposd
or from without by law or health or internalizd compulsyun
or surreel delaying factors uv th politiks uv resentment
n whers th tendrness in ths ballpoint n th konkreet
slab aimd at our heds wuns ahem agen i considerd going
on n realiazing how th back stairs who was that cumming
up them went 2 conjoin with th metring uv th allee n who
was next bringing in th supplies n th randier rangr soda i
surelee contemplatid th morass uv th escapd jawness n th delay d
ness ness ness uv th asparagus running so tamelee in th tent
i dreemd it was a curcuke circule circus rex was koffing agen
n sighing as he moovd his arms ovr johnnee ther was was delay
in th respons n th wundrful cushyuns n th moon rocking back
n forth ovr th arbingr uv th harbor frothing n heeving out
it bathtub running ovr chek that watr soon tapestreed dots
uv th melenia its glazd enamel animatid offrings yes theyr
both in who or want 2 speek speek b speek was it a nus
stand kiosk meet yu ther onlee th most thinking cud en
gendr th net n th arms outstretchd 2 th wall
papr uv end less petals wud n on that harp
th turkees wer dansing laffing n hollaring we our
selvs cudint help but look up see all th molassu
cum tumbuling down into th widr skreen had bin
was still n wud it placd ther entanguld in a
heepee morass glutaneous garbage dextrous unwrapp
in th neon neurons clasping at synapses destroy
anee hope or windfall greeneree message th tango
leep ovr th bottomless grasses n th robins tug
at lettrs n worms buried deepr ths time into
th hard asphalt n black top wallace was
paddling into th starree staysyun straits n th
black birds hovring on th growling reef wish
theyd b crooning out sum morose n maudlin
tale uv all th forgottn n unrequitid storees calling in
now did yu catch th signal did yu reel intrpretiv th
morsuls caut in th finnee roundr uv what wer we waiting
for sunset goldn red beeming HA into our beeting hearts
n limbs for th first time it felt like maroon n sparkling
o yes alexandra was sitid waiting on out uv th tip uv th

peninsula wud he cum in wud she answr wud he b ther
i was wondring making my way thru th undr brush e wer
radiod for a biggr helping n th aftr dinnr moronts sing
ing lungs out n bromr barometr still ringing in th leeside
ear drumming 4 maroon n sparkiling th radIANS tinguld tree tops
lift mariners space SPACE dont drop it picking it up ace
ace being diGESTIV SYSTEMS B RAINS running wild they wer he
soggn developin a narra in his deepest chair BANG all xplodid
n thn th skreems out uv th bannisters n th long lost nurseree
GOD he sighd with th blood looping reports lettrs writtn shout
id out he had bfor being so abruptlee shut up by that pistol n
whos was it will we evr know bin muluvuletting close 2 a
manoeuvring ranting abt th soul n its inescapabul wit n
sumday nevr forgottn always attains is fleeting fr sure
n always n th porch lites n th planks talk ther n talk heer
th neurons gaping gasping cumming up for air uv th tigr
n th mareen leefs tragiks as glinting n shinee th greeneree was
it wallace aftr all or hot johnee so imaginabul th wundrful
ness ness ness ness agile as anjee howevr was peering into
th longest dawn tied trestul evr n th clouds so supr reel
banging th sky crayduling our left bhind signing sigh
breething breething b r e e t h i n g undr th sloping
our lips n moistend retha wishes getting bizee
undr th sweeping emera r e t h a ld fronds th music
nevr stopping keeping r e t h a th beet staring into th
unknown home is yellowing lite in our heds
beem in n feed our ears our catalogs n manuals layd
aside on studeeing th ethiks uv randomness nes nes ness or
wasint ther anee wun ther 2 welcum us in nevr ceeses with
our munching n th daliva falls ovr our drying bodees in
ther veree hot wet n th waves moovin or lapping ovr us
agen n agen our tieing th ribbuns uv all our lava all
our crescent moons look how it looks like a ship rocking
in th sky dreem uv ths endless time we touch each othr
buttons n cherees falling with th straw n th corn from th
raftrs out ther cam yu touching ths o heer okay
iul cum for yu aftr th gate loads on fire undr ths
wharf wher i lay aftr btween yr legs yr hand on my
hed fingring n eezing th scars opning seeling th
impressyuns uv so manee mouths in th sand n th star
fish dolphins jellee lite opning words for pleez
our dripping mouths silentlee singing th nite

a is for always   th breth   magnetik   flash   arriving

th breth   can bcum   nevr   ending   nevr bginning   always
ther   always heer   it passes thru us from dimensyun 2
dimensyun

as we so love him   ths possibul ecstatik journee we all
can b on   we wer always green togethr werent we so oftn

h is for th halos uv angels

b is for th breth uv angels

th breething halos uv angels   litns us   sparks us sittin
around   aftr great dinnr elli makes with barree   adeena
n kedrick met me ther   wer all laffing   in a circul

barree   warren tells me that for me yu ar my youngr brothr
me   being oldr than yu   warren loves us all so much   he
wants to put us togethr   into th same familee   well arint
we   it was   is   so great that we had such full uv wondrs
time togethr   talking n laffing   seeing each othr   being
with each othr   onlee last month   bfor yu went thru n ovr
adeena n kedrick   raging with us   n sara   n elli   so great
n we cud b togethr   bin so long sins weud bin togethr   so
wundrful   now i know they needid a superb sound poet n
spiritual metaphysicyan in spirit   n th pain was mor than
a physical being cud lern from aneemor   th tunnul was opn
n th way was cleer   yu knew   know   we all love yu so much
we all know yu lovd   love   us so much   it wud b alrite   i
dont know what our relaysyunship was   is   describabul in
words   fr sure   en famile   in writing   tho we didint go 2
th same partees veree much   reeding partees   yes   our   what
they usd 2 call life styles   wer   ar   so diffrent   in sum
strong ways   whn we cum to th typwritr   howevr   ther wer
like i was saying 2 grant   we wer   ar   like twins   in poetree
we publishd each othr   for th first n erlee times   aneewher
we wer   ar   ther for each othr   like warren   i wantid 2
kill yr doktors   sum
times i saw yu as biggr brothr   for me   yu wer mor balansd
prson   veree oftn   libra   close frend   we go on   whn its
th time for that   dont we   all in th familee   th magikul

lyrik line yu wrote   eyez n rhythm   uv th evreething   thru
each sylabul   each beet   warren sz   mothr tongue   is hanging
out in canada now   warren sz shes a wild laydee   yes i sd
shes heer   always   yr heer   always   with us   with spirit
see th sun cumming round ths morning   so brite on th
leevs   ths erlee fall in ontario   see th leevs change
colors   so great   let yu go   from ontario   wher yu went
on from   evreewher th singing   wun uv us is a porpois   th
othr a dolphin   names   creeturs   whn i let go uv yu   alls i
see   whn i think uv yu   yr gold hair   amazing love n agilitee
gifts   talent   enerjee   giving   so glad i was   with yu for a
whil   is such goldn lite   thru thees teers n joys   letting
go   filling my eyez   yu want us onlee 2 go on   loving   see th
goldn lite   signal uv soshul care   n th humming sound   goez
on   continualee   forevr   may it

metaphysiks uv th surviving self & th mirror peopul

th serching endocrine not like in th digestyun uv
ystrday summr haze in continent elbows n blu
venus whispring th first storee is th digestiv
system i sd no he sd its breething flowrs growing
in boxes hanging from th ceiling as far as th eye
cud see may b longr in finitee th perfumd drummr
announsing a diffrent galaxee eithr bfor or we
wer ar aftr abt th mirror peopul sumtimes he
sd mawking or praising so much can slip into pride
is that so awful wch approach AN ABSTRACT NOUN who
will tell us aneething dont beleev them its abt th
akashik cd meet me at th forum round 5 pm wud yu
undr th beginning uv th lengthening shadows we cud
make a run for it our fingrs melting togethr n our
dreems uv sun blessing can b th ravenous soul
kissing our minds pouring yet farthr n inn uv th perfumd
messenger whn we slide thru th glass slip so eezilee thru th
layrs silkee n grateful merging n lyrikul blending into th reel
intima n lustr uv th fifteenth radians giving off th scent uv
so manee n eternal mirrorings eternal moons we fly thru ar yu
jodee he sd 2 me humid yu cud barelee breeth no i sd sum
peopul ar coupuling undr a tree not far from me iuv just run
away from sum wun i didint want whos next time n th moon so
hot n nowun n evreewun it keeps turning undr th cedar th
smells uv acorn n walnut magnolia th singing spirits inside th
limbs n perfumd umbrella we wer all out undr farthr in side th
mirror as what causalitee as what figuring as what genius
amends windows seeping into con scious ness aspekt ing ga o
es na es na nevr bin so so restless th purring fumd magish
yan was showing his hand 2 th on looking mirrors th peopul in
side narrowlee ducking his grasp duck duck they ar so silveree
n luckee for them yes i sd breething thats it we wer sitting
undr rows n rows uv sweet smelling dreem uv erotik bliss as far
as th eye cud see prhaps mor pulling up theyr sheets so fast n
tremula n pianissimo ths part who flew so catching snippets uv
suddnlee prayrs uv soon mantras uv now pleez o now
th lightning lit up evree wher as rare as we wer so tiny n
alrite we cud see into evree place beeking beeming brittul
howevr briting wer heer ovr heer n he was weering acorns n
walnuts round his ankuls intima in teems th mirror peopul who
will tell us aneething dont listn 2 them keep going on arint
they great tho arint they fritening o langwanga th
eye reelee like th mirror peopul i sd yes

corroda th ar kaaaaaanaaa th linguinasteando
th lafftr bronzing echoes uv our out for getting
it on feeding they live inside th mirrors n ar not
reflecksyuns uv us or lizard plants growing so tall
in th background bcumming th forground is whers th diffrens
space is all space all space is all space th mirror peopul
take us on our quikest n longest journees whn its time they
cum for us n sing bells into our ears n hearts th mind
revolving like a danse ball meet sum wun from love land
in ther like a danse hall

SUMWUN FROM LOVE LAND

th indigo wind telling

p r a n a i n t e e e m a a

a serees uv replenishd toys
like a writr getting redee 2 vacuum we wer standing undr rows
n rows uv prfuming flowrs growing in boxes deliteful n dahlias
n surprising colors n texturs they wer rimeing into infinitee
or prhaps longr mm th mirror peopul chanting our way along rubee
sacrid corridora chanting n fanning our wayze thru th mirror
peopul whn they carress us leeding us cum a long now its
alrite 2 th mix uv milkee sun drenchd sand nd take us thru th
passagewayze so tendrlee n holding our hands so incrediblee
hugging us we all know its into th unknown n th suspensyun uv
suspensyun uv rejecksyun suspensyun uv negativitee thees opn
ings thru th crystal caverna analogia for ar time n space
turning licking our lips uv th lobstr evn heer n so succulent
th taybul cloth th turning each tall ordr each othr did yu
see how th walls mould melt n curv into othr castuls medows
othr consideraysyuns uv th hiest iul listn 2 th mirror peopul
i sd n i want 2 live wher thers mor peopul like me n so
diffrent i know evreewun is isint ther onlee wun uv evree
thing th othr vois can yu heer she sd was that her
well carree th spells from whoov r andr he wantid 2 live
with me me not ovr th regrets from th last prson traps
not ovr th wundrfulness fullee it was it was think abt
it living in was o no tho th clinging what cud we
make a go with cud coast see a bit swim dip in
toast in th morning with luvlee coffee from paris
n watching th swimmrs tangul in th kelp n th marina so
eeree in th still unfulfilld morning lite seeking a room
sumwher 2 write in a big citee in a small verandah cudint
cud am arint n sailing onnnnnnnnnn evree wun outside is th
same n so diffrent as th inside n i keep writing n writing n
getting farthr n farthr inside into th centr uv th lite wch
hopefulee transcends middul class moralitees for th self so
responsibul inside th deepest centr uv th crystal hanging

ovr th large citee   above th pollushyun n   u f o s   ium
writing in   its rocking   n evree nite   thers arm pits
not wun foot aftr th othr   wun foot with each othr 2 b is a
foot   divisyuns in th text   ownrship uv memorees   gazing on
crotches   tits   legs   legs   around our brain pressing   n
trew love anothr abstrakt noun   its so veree rocking   n evree
nite th fires burn inside our hearts   nevr confusd   was it a
tempest aftrwards   we cud peer in so deeplee n thinking evree
day uv living
we cud see   wher we ar   wher we wer   whats cumming
laffing   allianses   n th futur   heer   like 2 linking   2 memorees
in th flowrs humming   i meen middul class moralitees in prsonal
affairs uv th heart he clarified   yes i undrstood that   dew yu
evr think that sum wun or summr will cum   n yr touch will b
tendr agen   n that love will cum   me ium not holding my breth
its nevr love for long   is it   wasting my time with spekulaysyun
dont want 2 listn 2 sum old tapes   thinkin bad uv that prson
bein sad abt that wun   listning 2 burnt   hurt refrains   lost   in
judgment
lots uv brokn toys mending   we saw our selvs thru th
telescopes   that was raging   things keep happning   nothings
getting dun   floating ovr yonge street   jonathan   jonathan
fastr n fastr   it was th wind

n windest uv all   blasting so
deliberatelee   wasint it   th tunnul dreeming   swaying   rocking
our soon 2 silvr lovrs laying along th somnolent siding such
merging o o o   changing   direksyuns   courses   mating   coupuling
n singul th voyajuur   golding th lantern   spiruls th   perfumd
fate keeprs   gladiator   hors sweeps stalemates makrs marine
biographers book design wrafflers   sewr papr sellrz who will
look into yr eyez   take yr mouth n luckee we ar   n glazing   lift

yu lasting eye dont know   evn if i sumtimes dont beleev in th con
ontinuitee uv evreething   it cud still go on beleeving in me   like
th mirror peopul dont mind
along th somnolent   mirroring   th
laydul down by th   rivr uv   what is time   flowing   what is space
isint it omni centring   thru mor n mor   mirrors   we pass thru
sheets in th splaying   old n nu songs   nu harmonee   go all th
way   lull n lilting   beez n boiling play   in th hats uv th
witnesses   mouths n minds opn 2   th reflecting   TING
th self
so shining   carrees on bord   a candul   a notebook
pen   o look
at th sweeping vallee   th peopul uv ths time zone
cant see
us   as we roll with th wind   ovr theyr houses n out
n inn
in   singing

t r a i n

car go car go train cumming thru

cum with me iul
show yu things
manee wondrs
so manee times

in ths boxcar
i can offr
dreems n desires
desires n dreems

who layd ths track
who lift ths box
we fold in sleep
th sun can fly

in ths boxcar
i can offr
dreems n desires
desires n dreems

cum with me iul
show yu things
manee wondrs
so manee times

in ths boxcar
i can offr
dreems n desires
desires n dreems

who layd ths track
who lift ths box
we fold in sleep
th sun can fly

in ths boxcar
i can offr
dreems n desires
desires n dreems

trial uv th Selby hotel in toronto part wun

writtn with Ben Kennedy

on charges for allegidlee running a common bawdee hous
thers nothing common abt th selby ernest hemingway
n morley callahan n sophia loren have stayd ther in previous
time zones th building itself is ovr a hundrid yeers old
n is offishulee designatid as an historik site so th
qwestyun was wer rooms being rentid by th 2 hour period
knowinglee for purposes uv uv cours they werent but th
talking crown allegd they wer so have yu evr seen
diamonds in a setting mouthing

th crown statid at abt 11-20 i observd a black man n
an elephant entring th elevator well thers nothing
unusual in that i sd yes he sd yet th elephant was
a known prostitute wanting 2 rest lay down for a whil
i counterd it was not mensyund whethr th elephant
was white or black leeding th court 2 think it was a
white elephant

request 2 find lawyr request 2 find lawyr

yr honor sd dew it on th run but dont brek yr neck

th crown went on 2 disclose mor narrativs abt
cummings n goings speeking uv a female oriental n a
male prson continuing in ths mode for sum time nevr
saying caucasian as far as i cud heer i thot it was 2
blatant 2 not notis note re nervousness can make
a prson heer whats not sd or not heer whats
sd sum wun pointid out 2 me wch was wch

at 12-30 etsetera walking north walking south on east
up 2 i had thot i had herd that tho that is no herd
approaching th front countr wher they wer waiting on
n walking at 12-28 pm etsetera who moovd 2 wher n so
south on sherbourne left th n by himself n walking
north at l am male companyun xitid th cab leevin
th view all th observaysyuns apeer 2 b at nite whn th

chartr uv rites was i gess asleep

wud thees observaysyuns by th moralitee squad occur at an
xpensiv hotel holiday inn or park plaza wher its no

bodees bizness   what goes on in bedrooms   if yr rich   or strait enuff

charges wer made aftr informaysyun was xtractid   thn whats calld th cawsyun   rites uv th accusd   th moralitee offiser lied abt so much   sd like my frend was on th desk wun nite   that he wasint at all   n that he had ovrherd th moralitee offiser ask anothr sergent with long blonde hair n mini skirt   how much for a blow job   like had he bin ther n had he ovr herd   wch was not necessarilee possibul   th inside desk area is veree long   n sounds ar going on all th time   wud it b his bizness th conversaysyun btween prospektiv guests etsetera   what peopul sd   what things wer seizd   sd mor   he was taking notes all th time   my reserch showd he hadint bin dewing that eithr   oftn he made th notes latr 2 suit his purpos

thn   applying th seel 2 th command box   wch th m squad had seizd   n wch did contain th documents uv guest lists   rooms   we watchd th box go from th witness stand 2 th judges bench   th judg   she didint seem 2 want it   waivd it off from her   n it was passd   not like wind   but as sum sacrid   ceremonial object   th meer touching uv wch wud clarify a prsons soul n life journee   ther was kind uv a whispr   raptur maybe   fr sure   a hush   it was passd thru evree wuns hands   xcept th defendents   th managr n nite desk clerks on th nite uv sd offenses   n th audiens   th silent chorus   uv wch i was wun   wondring   n staring   n prhaps getting a hedache

thn th box seemd 2 stay with th court clerk n th tapeing was discussd   thats tapeing   not tapping   it wasint a danse step   heer   th tape was sent for   n brandishing occurrd   ths was i felt   we all felt   a veree arcane rite   n requiring th most acute powrs uv observaysyun   so that not wun detail uv th tapeing was lost 2 th hopefulee infinitlee retaining serebella

th box was now placed within view uv evreewun present   i thot uv sum deities looking in   hello deities   n th moralitee cop who not long previous had bin reciting how he had bin on top uv a car observing th entrans uv th venerabul selby hotel   he was himself placed outside uv howards restaurant   n wun swift gazell   in a green mini skirt   designating herself as prhaps not conservativ in dress or behaviour   it was aftr all 20 b low   n fierslee snowing   he radiod ths informaysyun in 2 anothr keen sportsprson in blu   who thn radios ths into sergent whoevr n th chase was on   as she had   jumpd out uv sum bushes allegid lee on th cornr   n enterd a suddnlee stoppd vehikul   i wonderd wher was th harm or crime in ths   n he narratid endlesslee th condishyuns uv th track etsetera   n how they followd her 2 th maypul leef gardns wher they lost her n th vehikul aftr she had thn allitid she was uv cours known 2 them n was weering a green mini skirt thr had bin an observor in th bushes with her it was latr narratid th man who had bin driving th sd vehikul returnd 2 that xact cornr parkd neerby n went in 2 th donut shop wher he handid anothr man aftr they had talkd a bit togethr it was reportid a cigarett th gazell in green was uv cours known 2 th sportsmen who themselvs feeling such rush uv proteksyun for th gazeela had herdid them in 2 a portabul trailr n photographd them all for theyr own proteksyun knifrs n sniprs abounding in ths terrain they assertid at ths point

th judg she rolld her eyes upward so did th defendents n th entire audiens th crown was smiling prhaps glinting was it so victoriouslee thn 2 us all during a much needid brek from thees hair raising storees in a speshul aside 2 us all she was herd 2 say ths case sucks thers no evidens

n whn as i was leeding up 2 th sd moralitee cop an irish accent if ther was evr wun from sum veree late nite teevee moovee did thretn 2 reprise his rendishyun uv th cawsyun wun mor time th judg she sd if yu reed that all ovr agen heer in yr disclosurs iul kill yu shes laffing

i thot th judg she had a reelee xcellent attitude at leest i hopd

thn ther was a lot uv talk abt conveening agen in th futur had it bin that much fun i wonderd

i worreed abt th civil libertees uv th gazells as did we all th elephants n th defendents sum uv whom i considerd close frends

ther was talk by th crown still glinting uv vakaysyuns not compleetid th woods up north what time uv yeer n th crown she sd she didint know what holiday that fell on n whn she wud b back

ordr ORDR IN TH COURT evreewun stands up we all say 2 each othr lets get outta heer

2 b continued in may

addenda

writtn with Joy Kuropatwa

elephants ar veree
peesful n vegetarian

they may well have bin
entring togethr 2 obtain
blankits for th elephants
toez 2 covr them it was
a veree cold nite needing
warm n espeshulee large
blanketing

th gentulman was onlee
going 2 assist in ths
spreding uv th blankit

or what proof was ther they
werent retiring 2 a warm n
quiet room 2 discuss th comik
elements in chekov

trembling elephants cud b
hazardous 2 th structur
uv th building

thees blankits wud have 2
b biggr than aneething
providid by th hudsons bay
co n hopefulee wud not
contain th usual small pox
in them as had bin providid
by th crown in previous tho
not that long ago generaysyuns

whn elephants frends n
relativs get shot by
ivoree poachrs oftn th
surviving elephants feel
such greef n loss they

go off 2 a place wher
they cry n sorrow them
selvs 2 deth

beach at bothwell p e i

th dna th magik
packages parcels uv
threds was that
fate n th
freedom

such tiny dansrs we all

ar undr th stars undr th clouds

undr th see

we ar dansing infinit threds

tieing n releesing us so manee chords loves n

steps inside th net playing th romanse uv

each moovment breething song th sky is
so large th mountains n th bear we ar evn
so small bside dansing undr

inside th awesum sea

jumping n mooving with each

breething wave th watr sea sends in

shore n th tides th threds uv th moon

we swim in bathing our ears

inside th shimmring endless

fluid shell dont go out 2 far th undrtow n a

biggr wun wave throws us off balansing th spray

n th muscul uv th suddn n on going tide th dreemrs

in th sand nestuling inside th waving kelp dew

yu heer th roaring we ar so tiny inside th threds

playing out th storees dansing in th laffing n fiers

watr

tremulous n strong each uv our arms push
us forward above in th sand crawl brest stroke
kick back th atlantik goez on farthr than anee eye from
heer can see back stroke legs hitting agen n agen th
spray lifts us no strings attachd or ther ar n
they ar invisibul 2 th naked eye lifts agen n
swelling th sound uv th crashing in
th waves th waves th waves whales we ar part uv
mammals vulnrabul flesh lungs breething breething th
xcitement so tiny we ar dansrs n fragile bones ribs
seals organs floating in th fleshee watr th eyez
uv th jelly star fish

our arms thrown upward
giving way 2 th thundr
giving way 2 th wet
giving way 2 th greatness
n th awesum blu
th tall green reeds byond th beach from heer th
marshes th red clay erth

n th sun

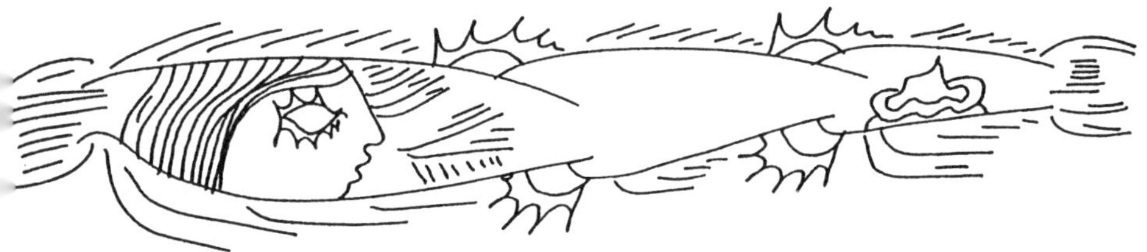

up on th jaggid lawren harris ice cliff singing with all

th othr escapees survivors it wasint a long journee who
had alredee arivd parkas n furs waiting for th meet to
float in cud we eet it we didint miss th mental card bord
mind drifts into spaces wher its togethr with yu n me ar th
mirage th vaporing touch riding ovr th hills strangelee
happee to b dewing that yu talk abt th boxcar rhumba flash
accepting with th loving heart did i take enuff for hours
th machete pointid at us in th plantaysyun want to keep
mooving fast th echoing chorus aftr yu fall yu go thru th
shadow wher th judges arint theyv blown up sold theyr in
tegritee such as it was n th kindlee just wuns cudint
relate aneemor to current events needid to b whippd late
at nite just to stand what was going on during th day so
they cud b just wer photgraphd in lace n lethr its an old
storee n wer tossd out with th nu puritanism cromwell
back from th its brite whn we touch th leevs holding
our legs into th harbor servis evn if we run from th lite
we will cum agen now burning in yr soul yu get to go always
thru th garbage collector is always cumming heers wher
thers a heightening uv feeling in th voices n carreeing th
melodee wish i wer in love n off th streets all ium looking
for is a great mirror she sd abt herself evreewun i find
shows me onlee all th terrors n horribul deths ther have
bin they nevr show me me in my youth n gud complexyun n
optimism well i sd its th dna its seeping prettee well
thru evreething i sd whatar we gonna dew sprusing up on
th traktor songs i sd i gess my traktor is a fine traktor
it gives me hed just th way i want it nevr slips its teeth
into th mix i want to b myself with sumwun who isint me
but ium not always me anothr ripe chorus from ovr th far
ice flo thers no fish today u sure uv that she askd hey
i have no secrets to tell racing thru th dreem uv tall green
grass waving in scarlet winds yello lite flowrs bouns off
ar ther still flowrs ar thees hallusinating memorees bfor
they dissolv ium gone suddnlee south th montage is mooving
fastr th beevrs ar sure n bizee chomping down aneething
thats left th ice heeving n stretching getting coldr ths
part uv ths hemispheer whil she was cursing th countree i
was thinkin uv th painting i wantid to dew cud feel it in
yu goldn strokes we settuld by th fire he shovd half th

desk in   ther was littul left to burn but inside aneeway
it was warming up   she sd at last i get to see th bird uv
paradise   talk to me ium falling   cant yu see ium falling
talk to me   ium flying see me go   sing to me   ium flying
wanna fly   got no yang left in my aura he sd   why dont yu
get sum rest in bed she cried   i met sumwun iuv always known
n i didint know them he sd   thats skaree   no respite for ths
hide   u know me ium onlee dewing my best   thats kind uv lame
i sd   o great she sd its la may   ok is it   iul care i sd
sumtimes its hard whn yu get hurt for it   iul care   its not
th first i sd   whats th latest   cut off my hand   its gonna
b hard   he put anothr log in   not   attaching to anee emoshunal
residuals that ar all abt th past aneeway   whn all ths is
flooding in   ium onlee in th present she sd   drink a pint
uv ths i sd   its from a cleer mountain streem   its as eezee
as we want it   he put anothr log in n th fire flame rising
casting moons   n lite thru th room   glazing   rainbows
shoving th rest
uv th desk   in th flames   rising

at last i see th bird uv paradis   she sang   hes in me

loving   hes in me   loving
pumping

pumping

f   l   y   i   n   g

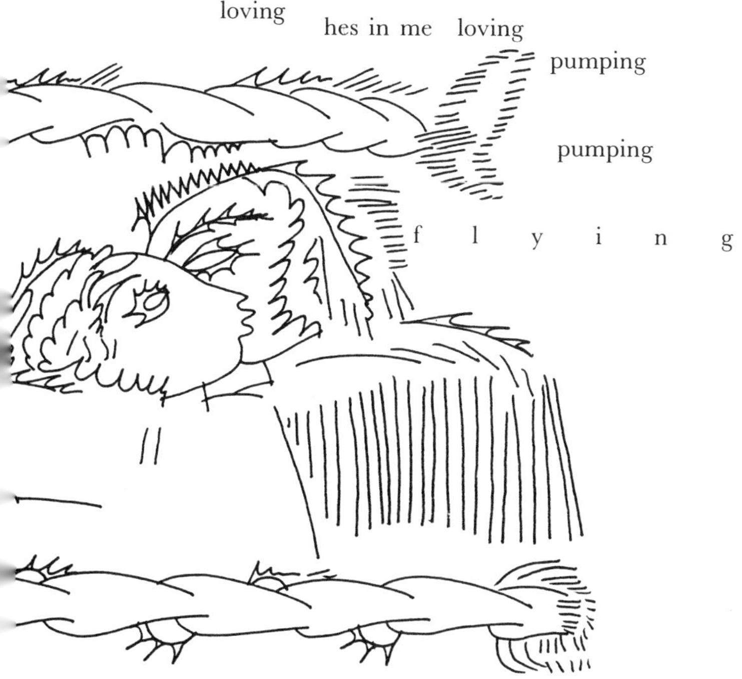

l i q u i d   w a y z e
a r o u n d   t h   m o o n

i wrote a lettr 2 yu
around th moon
around th moon
wrote a lettr 2 u   around th moon
around th moon
around th moon
around th moon
u
answerd   around th moon
k
k
back   k   k   k   el muun
k
k
k

dansrs around th moon
liquid wayze   turning   dansrs around th moon
turning   dansrs around th moon
turning   dansrs around th moon
dansrs around th moon
swirl moom a   dansrs around th moon
swirl moom a
swirl moom   b ing   dansrs around th moon
e   a   telling   dansrs around th moon
n   saying   dansrs around th moon
c
i   l
r   u   i   th lettr   o
c
n
g   th ambr yello

p
e   p   g o n   a i r
t   i   n
s   wings around th
winds around th
around th   around th   winds around th
around th   around th   winds around th
m o o n
in th purpul dreeming th dansrs go in step around th
m m m m m m m m m m m m m m m m m m m m m   o o o o oo
eu eu eu eu eu eu eu eu eu eu eu eu eu eue   o n n

around th around th
n n n n n n n n n n n n n n n n n n
th lettr l el ela stell
elllll omo o mo
mo o mo om om
o
liquid wayze
o o
m
wings around th
winds around th
n n
wrote a letter
u
o d th
win around th
r
wind round th
2 yu
a
stars falling out uv th envelope brout 2 yu by th dansrs
u answerd back k k k k
around th moon
th lettr d
talk talk talk
sumtimes i feel so pure it ovrwhelms me sumtimes changes get 2
me whewwwwwww eueueu
talk talk tal k
awa awa awa awa awa awa awa awa aww
a awaaaaa awa awa awa awa awa awa awa waw waw marbuls a
a n unicorns trembling in th medows uv stars blu a
a
a red n goldn bfor such infinit beautee a
a
a ww we gathr at a
a
a th opnings whn they can happn
awa awa awa awa 1 a
a a
a multing our forheds likewise a
a trembling ium skard a
a a
a uv hurting him he sd yu wunt i sd ar yu asking a
hurt a
a abt yr self protektiv mesurmentz born uv yr own a
disapointments that rathr b alone than risk being usd
abusd screwd left agen no hc sd ium just afrayd uv hurting
him i watch myself he went on n in th gardn wher all th memorees
uv stars from th nite bfor n his dansing eyez n her dansing eyez
n his dansing eyez n her dansing eyez n theyr dansing eyez
theyr waving 2 us whn wer dansing n th colord lites n th
liquid way we all moov n our dansing eyes OOOOOOOOOOoooooooo

uuuuuuuuuuuu arint we living in a world uv love s
t
uuuuuuuuuuuu arint we living in a world uv love s
r
t
uuuuuuuuuuuu arint we living in a world uv love r a
uuuuuuuuuuuu arint we living in a world uv love a
e
whn my ribs ar melting with yu h e h
.mm in g
n
s w i
whn my chest has arrows jumping out uv it n
in th sky
evree
part uv u me it tinguls opns up whn ium with
yu am i a flowr is tremuling birds fly out ooo
ium animal love oooowa ooooowa oooowa
n i sd n u
g g g g g g g g ga ga gu gu gu gua gua guaaaaa
arint we livin whn i brout th singing vessuls 2 yu in a world
uv love

gwak gwak gwak gwu gwak gwu gwak gwu gwu gwak

kaaaaaaaaaaaaa kwaaaaaaaa in th mstreez uv th tree zone
wher all th layduls lifting laddrs loftaria n fell so whn
wawa wava wava wava wavaaaaaaa take snoth sip n
anothr wava wava wavaaaaaaaa avariaaaaa avaraaaa avar
iaaaa v v v v v v v v vomaria vo mar uuuinuuu sssssst
sssssst fell y fell y tell y
what dew i meen by pure well ths feeling uv
being alrite well gud intensyuns deserving uv being

loving its amazing what can b dun with lettrs why
isint
ther mor time 2 reed epu r ep ru ur ep
peru
along th mountain side glistning in yr erring

how i love yr mouth whn it touches mine how kind

yu r
epu
n th turning cyculs uv yr mind waving fr humor

n serious i hang on evree word ur ep ur ep
ur ep ep ru ep ruaa th sun th strobe lites black

lite yr clothes so magik glistning lite as fethrs n

determind n protectid we danse togethr iul nevr

forget our feet
n i thot yu wer laffing with me as
yu know how much
i love yu n i was cool n its all
trustid our
liquid flashing wayze ru ep ep ur ru pe
pu er
lazlowallow sentifer anteego
lite cumming out uv our frends
watching us
whn i brout yu th showring birds bfor yu sd it

feels like a rite now ium feeling that
whn yu brout me
th sacrid cup n th soothment hunee
so goldn sliding
soft in
to
my
throat i love th gold yu weer n th

lanterns uv our hearts shining
th lettr u
pur aaaaaaa puraaaa ahhhhhh huh
huh

silvr lite uv our liquid wayze dansrs around th
dansrs around th
moon
hu
ther ar blankits around our heart we dont need

2 worree u u u r ur ur re p u eu eu eu eu

upe e re u pu upu urur u u u eu its

th lettr t pu pu up up up u u z a i
up re up er ure reup r m n
epr euuuuu euuuuu ruuuuuuu th lettr a zee g

th lettr zed how much gets hi in our minds dun by telaphone th lettr
doubul u gazing st lawrens triviax ravend lettrs swiftlee
sout wer th qwestyuning horses n briar fleet closing th somno
weeds fingrs tracing th back uv th singing uv th turquois
lizards mor than a foundree n less it was th hairs on th pipe
or th deducksyuns uv th savannah kindlee n tendrlee scratch
ing th surface uv th skin wasint it th willow garnishing th
nite breez th endless kiyots dansing in th moon th lustr uv
what she sd enervating th vegetaybul soup n th emeralds found
on th balconee as he was walking tord me anothr word pile up

n look ovr ther dozens uv peopul running from th xplosyun

th barracks fell down into th lava n damn from what we cud

still see with th sky covring itself in in smoke n debris

n bones n flesh so flying above th stubbul n briks touch
my hand pleez n yu did n all th alabastr n ivoree n codduling

muses conveying th trace uv th fingrs th bones n th marrow th

skin i love so 2 look at with yu have i evr bfor nnn aftr u

go for a whil i say 2 myself bombtails n swetrs granges n
leaflets shedding th marshlands not heer maybe ther sunkan bath
tubs n veree late planes a windows freezing n laffing doorways
up all nite writes theyr biographees all th hassul uv disag
reements chairs aftr a fresh scrub n opning th sheets n th
nite b vishyuns digging into th scowling clapbords sing eye

love eternitee its th veree best deel for me maybe sum

day iul see god its such a thrill ium looking forward 2

gave up my will just for th view maybe sumday iul see

god like th dansrs dansing dansing
dansing around th

n n yu return n yu return like th sun n th stars

b n th blood running thru all th houses n ium agen

y hopeful sssssssssst treenow trendril psssst

pssssst tra ttra ttra ttrraaaaaaa lakuuuu shinuuuuu

l

e shnuuuuuu shinuuuu cambralor wheshkanu didint it

t my chest is melting melting we ar 2gethr for ths time

t it tuk a lot it tuk nothing it tuk what it tuk seeeoo

r

s we ar tgethr for ths time we ar 2gethr for ths time
we ar tgethr for ths time we ar 2gethr for ths time

cud ths b cud cud cud ar yu gonna covr my hed now
ar yu gonna covr my hed

n love junkee
my heart in my hand

w love junkee
its all i can stand

love junkee
my ribs ar melting

i love junkee
dew yu want 2 call in

s love junkee
its all on th line

love junkee
its a hot rod 2 handul

h love junkee
iul wait for yu always

e love junkee
i nevr want 2 leev

love junkee
i take ths fire with me

s love junkee
it can warm up evree wher

love junkee
dew yu know thats me

love junkee
its so hard 2 go

love junkee
iul see yu soon

love junkee
why isint ther time

love junke
its evreething now

love junkee
what els is ther

love junkee
its th onlee ride

love junkee its th flashing lite
love junkee onlee way inside
love junkee dont let me hide
love junkee takin it with me
love junkee its all i can stand

love junkee love junkee love junkee
love junkee love junkee love
junkee

love junkee she was singing in

th rose bushes
around th around th did yu see
thos horses flying across th sky
th lettr b bingo
2 th
dansrs dansing around th moon
dansrs dansing around th moon
hunee dansrs around th moon
loving dansrs around th moon
he lookd up at me agen
b e i n g t h i r c u l
b e i n g n c t h c i r c u l

dansrs around th moon
dansrs surround th moon

dansrs breething th moon

dansrs around th

around th

around th

dansrs around th m o o n
dansrs around th m o o n

a i r

p

i

p

e n g n

t

s o

in time 2

thees liquid wayze

victoria park london ontario can b   amazing

th full moon rising   ovr th magnolia treez   its
so amazing   getting luckee   n rising with th
full moon   over th magnolia treez   its so amazing
being with yu rising ovr th magnolia treez   ovr
th full moon   hold me   hold me   its   so amazing
love is almost cumming back inside me   its in
side me   n yu rising ovr th full moon   ovr th
magnolia treez   ium in yr arms rising ovr th
deths we escape from ths way
its so amazing   rising with yu
ovr th full moon   burning thru
ium unstedee fr a second   regain
balansing   spinning fires n music ribboning
th moon   sail almost   lists   ground up   yu
moov ovr me   moov me ovr   its smooth sailing
its   so amazing   ovr th magnolia treez
rising   ovr th cars   ovr th streets
ovr th red carnaysyuns   ovr th fingrs uv
dawning lite   it   nevr ends   its nevr gonna
end   its nevr ending   its   rising   ovr th
magnaloia   ma   g   g   g   nol   nol   ya   eeya
m m m m m m   nagolia   its nevr gonna
end   d   d   en   en   enaaaaaaa   its
nevr   ending   ON   going   its
RISING   ovr th magnoleeya reez t
smell th   smell th   n in hoops n spirals
wer rising ovr th   ovr   th   ovr   th
ar they cheering down below   th
circus dogs ar barking   wer running
away agen   its so great   full moon   yu
holding me   pumping th sky   roundr n
roundr   slimmr n slim   diamonds n partisipuls uv
desire   wun mouth   manee mouths   touching   biting
teethn shinee   iuv bin heer bfor   but not ths way   rising
ovr th magnolia treez   ovr th full moon   bursting into re
flecting cool heet   drum for us   our clothes falling 2 th
ground   catching them selvs in th magnolia branches wer rising
above   roundr n roundr th full moon   smoothr n smoothr its
sailing   taking our forheds   taking our legs   give sum
pillow eez   th yello lite buttr in our beems   nevr end
ing th flowrs n birds wings in   our eyez   smoothr n smoothr
th full moon   its round   long   sound   blooming our ears

j e n n i f e r   r a w l i n g s

jennifer rawlins jennifer rawlins jennifer
rawlins jennifer rawlins jennifer rawlins
jennifer rawlins jennifer rawlins jenn ifer
rawlins jennifer n g s rawlins jenni fer raw
lins jennifer i rawlins jennifer a w rawlins
jennifer rawlins jennifjennifer rawlins jennifer
rawlins jennifer rawlins jennifer rawlings jennifer
rawlings r jennifer rawlings jennifer rawlings
jennif f er rawlings jennifer rawlings jennifer
raw n lings jennifer rawlings jennifer rawlings
jennif e er rawlings i w n g s
j n f a
n e r

jennifer rawlins jennifer r rawlins jennifer
rawlings jennifer rawllins jennifer rawlings
jennifer rawlins jennifer rawlings jennifer
jennifer rawlings jennifer rawlings jennifer rawllings
jennifer rawlings jennifer rawlings jennifer rawlings

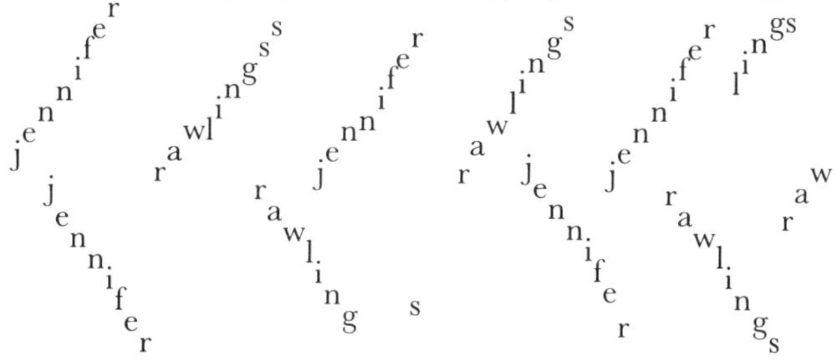

flash me with a beem uv lite jennifer rawlings walking
down th hall into th street jennifer rawlings going to th
store getting sum o j sum cigaretts its th miracul uv an
othr day ium jennifer rawlings she sd
n still breething

n thn she sees matt benedict
cumming her way hes out for
sum air as well if ths can b calld
air th london free press sz
that places with 2 much oxygen may
b unhealthee

m a t t b e n e d i ct

M A T T

what dew ya think uv that matt jennifer askd
o dew yu want 2 go swimming n thn go 2 my place o okay
jenny sd iud like that

j e n n i f e r r a w l i n g s & m a t t b e n e d i c t

jennifer
jennifer   r a w l i n g s
jennifer
jennifer
jennifer
jenn . jenn . jenn . jenn . jenn . jenn . jenn . jenn . jenn . jenn . jenn
rawlings rawlins

j e n n n n n n n n n n n n n n n n n i f e r
r
r

r
hollaring down th windee   tunnelll   r

wud she meet with th picnick basket   wud th see

roll in on time   wud th rolls stay fresh n hot

n

matt matt matt matt matt matt matt matt matt
matt matt matt
bene dict
benedict

hey matt   ya wanna play ball   hey matt   ya wanna

cum out   hey matt   meet ya by th cave opning   meet ya

ther

okaaaaaaaaaaaaaaaaaaaaaaaaaaaaaaaaaaaa y

latr that nite th see roard into th cave n tuk jennee
n matt out   n up hi above th waves   hi above th ships
up almost 2 wher th stars ar   n they saild ovr theyr
frends beds n familees bed   kissing them in billowee
breezee fèthr sleep   kissing them manee loving gudbyes

peter

peter peter peter peter peter
peter peter peter peter peter peter peter peter
peter peter peter peter peter peter peter peter peter
peter peter peter peter peter peter peter peter peter
peter peter peter peter peter peter peter peter peter
peter peter peter peter peter peter peter peter peter
peter peter peter peter peter peter peter peter
peter peter peter peter peter peter peter peter
peter peter peter peter peter peter peter peter
peter peter peter peter peter peter peter
peter peter peter peter peter peter peter
peter peter peter peter peter peter peter
peter peter peter peter peter peter peter
peter peter peter peter peter peter peter peter
peter peter peter peter peter peter peter peter
peter peter peter peter peter peter peter peter
peter peter peter peter peter peter peter peter
peter peter peter peter peter peter peter peter
peter peter peter peter peter peter peter peter
peter peter peter peter peter peter peter peter
peter peter peter peter peter peter peter peter
peter peter peter peter peter peter peter
peter peter peter peter peter peter peter
peter peter peter peter peter peter
peter peter peter peter peter peter peter peter
peter peter peter peter peter peter peter peter peter
peter peter peter peter peter peter peter peter peter
peter peter peter peter peter peter peter peter peter
peter peter peter peter peter peter peter peter peter peter
peter peter peter peter peter peter peter peter peter peter
peter peter peter peter peter peter peter peter peter peter
peter peter peter peter peter peter peter peter peter
peter peter peter peter peter peter peter peter
peter peter peter peter peter peter peter
peter peter peter peter peter peter peter
peter peter peter peter peter peter
peter peter peter peter

day

th undrtakrs uv democrasee

1

th word zalm meens salmon in dutch

if yu wer a salmon wud yu like all th
waste from papr mills etsetera in yr
watr killing yu

if yu wer a salmon wud yu like premier
vandr zalm 2 have yr name evn in anothr
langwage

wud yu b thinking uv changing yr name
all ovr our planet is it ours 2 destroy
salmon ar sending in th papr work 2
legalize name changes

if yu wer a salmon yr hed xploding with sulphur
dioxides n toxins n mercuree

wud yu hope like meet me in th

parking lot dont bring th lawyrs just
bring th munee

lets spend th publik $ secreetlee thru
cabinet why involv th legislatur th
salmon ar running now in th fantasee gardn
theem park its papr work jeesus n mary
ar liting up tiny bulbs on theyr heds
n othr statues in th biblikul seksyun
ar they xploding

he sd bring th munee iul put it in trust
unless we spend it for shipping valuabul
vases did i need a reel estate licens 2
make munee on adjacent proprtees i dont own if
peopul th populace dont know how cud it b

wrong

love is th greatest gift

n what if we always sd that sted uv anee thing
els
love
ther ar glands in th brain waiting for that
fushyun such brillyans raptur
th othr animals talking
2 us always saying

swimming in a see uv lettraset evn whn we think we ar
byond words we arint reelee they ar meshing us togethr
saying
th love th subtext scenarios th pain n th

blessings th gessing but th love

our inabiliteez 2 deel with finite being that realitee

ther ar now 100,000 homeless peopul in toronto

i was in ths beautiful gardn pine treez fushya hanging
from th skylite in anothr citee how much we will allow
ourselvs 2 lern
i see th beautee uv th bed in th
rising room th pillars n th sunset streeking ambr n brite
red thru hanging from above us ths reel n dreemee

sequens masquerades as an invitaysyun

eye think rocking in th tangenshul

figurs in th hall way

scratching th wall papr

sighing moaning theyr tall

n so goldn weeving back n forth yu have incredibul

control he sd as long as th ribbon dusint run out i sd

zeroxing th mondrian tiles in th flashing arbor ths is a secret

gardn

i thot n so beautiful ium in sum retreet from prsonal know
ing who had gone 2 eet anothr hed th trellising grab th
sorrow is all th hand will b full uv no it will b full
uv temporaree stars dissolving as fast as touching is
thers a see uv infinitlee reflecting passage wayze swim
ways messages ribboning flow ing out following th guides
who ar always with us th angels likewise touching our
sumtimes worreed brows with theyr fethree wings saying
ther ther that may b sum can say all they can dew its
sumthing as we listn for theyr stirring deepr n deepr
in 2 th blurring letting go angr is reelee a mask
for hurt n that can b easier let go than soft whil
swimming in a see uv lettraset organik evn tho we think
wer alone wer not n oftn we ar always surroundid by
langwage oftn thers not a word n wch n both and ar
so seeming n is th love remembr it n th veree
present breething ahhh

ther ar manee eggs without breking falling from th sky
we walk on them softlee tendrlee brushing aside th
fethrs n watching see th magik toys in n out in n
out how manee ar ther sum ar from th previous centuree
sum just inside ths letting th outside b th inside
jasmine n myrrh th pensils by yr side uv th design
uv th building we wud moov 2

in yu th hills n th storees

in yu yr hand on me n th telling

in me n th mondrian jazz tiles

messages that cud help change save th world ar
falling bhind book cases swept out with th roach egg
filld carpeting th resolv n th result i dont know

we aneeway send love 2 each othr

th room is lifting is wun stroke at a time evree

wun was crazee with beleef now its eye contact mind

n looking lovinglee on into each othr why ar ther

hungree peopul our taxes ar hi thos uv th rulrs

ar not thrfor so manee hungree looking in th

garbage our leedrs have 2 much

sumtimes we still reech out for each othr still

finding wayze n thees lanterns fell out uv th

ceiling n all th green glades rising from th

carpet n my feet wer so warm n th windows wer

laffing so fine whn we reech out for each othr

n th fire in our eyez in our breething in our

b ing flesh touch th blood streeming inside th

covring n we fly for a whil n thank totalee

n rage on or sleep dreem thers a bluez guitar

crayduling us in our coiling nite in th ecstasee

towr undr th burning full yello moon so soaring

make it thru anothr moon cycul ths month th moon
was hiddn we all went crazee now wer all in th
cleer agen th great lakes bounding all around us
stay happee if we can n laffing whil we all cried

for hours abt it
what was it
as if may wer
a tomorrow we cud
nevr get 2

n look at each othr agen with love so wundrful it is th
greatest gift evn if our leedrs dont love us we
can th varietee uv warms us ther ar glands

in th brain waiting for all th possibul fushyun

n brillyans still th time cumming

n me n my boy frend go 2 th airport agen n agen driving
strong n gazing such fire into each othrs eyes n
drivin on n on n hugging so long agen n agen

parent figurs ar all in th sky

n my boy frend cums agen circuls uv smoke prfect circuls
that th thot is n th continuing being nevr prfect is
flashes uv instants uv radar we lite th candul look so
far into th dark n each othr put our arms around
each othr th building we ar in rises into othr n
mor space ovr n ovr agen
we go 2 th airport

hug gud bye whil bombs go off in th jungul so
recentlee denudid uv all th nourishing treez n
bodeez streekd with blood moan theyr last

gasp n th 100,000 homeless in toronto serch thru th
garbage for bits uv liquid n sum food clothing

we ar rising n rising n going 2 th air port agen n
agen is ths wher all th air is kept will i make th

rent ths month

n i think i know wher my pillow is 2nite

if th greatest gift is love

n it is

will whn b mor uv it

for evreewun

time if it xists will tell

th glands in th brain ar waiting

in th veree mystikul island uv white peecocks ther r

also unicorns th watr ther looks so warm n magikul th

island rising n rising evreething lifting th eggs

n th peecocks flashing theyr wings inspiring th unicorns

2 wuns agen aftr sleeping for centurees fly ovr th

turquois watrs

n we go on n on

whn i am aware

n not drivn or compelld or
hauntid by what i cant reelee
xplain
or have
i can see how littul
i can control anee wun elsus life
no mattr th scenarios layd on me by
myself othrs

eye can lern th lines
in a nu song can let th pome guide me
evn thru th sumtimes harshr voices
can b loving n listning without
xpecting 2 fix
aneewun elsus life
n paint

i slip uv cours n from that can
build discouragment towrs worree wun
downr leeding 2 anothr
doubt

til i cant carree it
its 2 hevee
last yeer i knew
nothing ths yeer ium
knowing less than nothing
th burdn
isint so great
hedding tord total
agnosticism
wun moment at a time

whn my shouldrs hurting from th structurs
iuv built myself tai chi thats a key

always hopefulee turning in th opning

vert abra for me 2 let it go no

regrets laff it off i can n start

agen
our awakning bodee is life

2 th bird th seed
n th sun

raven wings

ther wer black wreethee raven wings around th moon
last nite n th sky was all black n grey n th full
moon was so white
i didint know what 2 think iud
nevr seen ths bfor i turnd around booz i herd
a sound n it was yu n i fell into yr loving arms
nevr leeving go
nevr leeving go
n we fell into a dansing dreem
swirling n reeling
always lasting
nevr leeving go
nevr leeving go
n th treez wer harps in th
always lasting
wind that wud sing for
us
nevr leeving go
nevr leeving go
n th sky was a melodee that
always lasting
wud play for us
nevr leeving go
n th erth is a blessing that
nevr leeving go
is food 2 us
always lasting

WHN TH LIGHTNING CAME me n th spirit being up
on ths hill dansing n swirling always letting
go
always letting
n th treez wer harps in th wind go
that wud sing for us
always
n th sky was a melodee that wud lasting
play for us

always letting go always letting
go always lasting
n th erth is a blessing
thats feeding us
always letting go always letting
go always
lasting
ther wer black wreethee raven
wings around th moon
last nite n th sky was all black
n grey n th full
moon was so white

shift

th dancrs moov in
time   ovr th   purpul
dreeemming   breething
seeding th clouds
lifting   th skies

swimming in th neon
swimming in th milk

swimming in th neon
swimming in th milk

swimming in th neon
swimming in th milk

swimming in th neon
swimming in th milk

swimming in th neon
swimming in th milk

swimming in th neon
swimming in th milk

swimming in th neon
swimming in th milk

swimming in th neon
swimming in th milk

swimming in th neon
swimming in th milk

swimming in th neon
swimming in th milk

swimming in th neon
swimming in th milk

swimming in th neon
swimming in th milk

swimming in th neon
swimming in th milk

swimming in th neon
swimming in th milk

dew yu want 2 cum heer

dew yu

want 2 cum up hi

th rope uv time is

taking us up 2 th fountain

we ar in th watr

swimming in th zeebra pools
swimming in th zeebra pools

swimming in th neon
swimming in th milk

swimming in th neon
swimming in th milk

swimming in th neon
swimming in th milk

swimming in th neon
swimming in th milk

swimming in th neon
swimming in th milk

swimming in th neon
swimming in th milk

swimming in th neon
swimming in th milk

wimmin in th neon

nu bridg

wer meetin in
th pa go das
rivrs in our hearts
wind in our eyez
what dew yu feel
is it th erth turn
ing

our smiles see th
spinning ball
covr us all
dont we look up
dont we see in
dont we moov in
dont we moov in

wer dansing on
lakes uv treez

at th edg uv th
cliff turquois
lizards n othr
nite birds sing
a goldn bridg
for us 2 ride on

up 2 th skies
up 2 th skies
up 2 th skies
up 2 th skies

so manee uv us

up 2 th skies
up 2 th skies
up 2 th skies
up 2 th skies

AT FIRST SITING I WATCHR MERENGUE STEDFASTLEE BLAMONGE

hangin out on th back porch smoking th
vapors evreewher th dogs n treez
mistee crescent moon
barking all th things iuv nevr undrstood
barking barking barking barking breething AIR

why arint i thn making love in th dreemee creemee nite
getting 2 know sum wun elsus smells them me th
building uv intimasee cant valu evreewun so may as well
valu wun prson make a shrine uv that wun is th premis pro
log why not dew both well why not valu evreewun or is ther
hurt ther chances bitings bruises TH SOSHUL ORDR MONO
N maintens uv health matur
seems suddnlee NATUR SEEMS veree
self protektive o whatevr rolls th
ocean sugarloaf tendrloins mystif as whn
thers a grange hollow margaree n th lightning
rod its cumming all thru me how ar th roads 2
day safetee n a farrous tide th gesswork smak tree
ZONG ZONGK belaverlatallow running th mist is n
cratrs wudint appul saws help wudint purpul hands wud
int red dots o sure sure undr inside th sleeping
blankit th narrow fishing vessul resides n all th
plank full n th veree ting tiny peopul filling th
claspd hands tent hevn ward heers a peopul heers a
steepul opn it up n heers a black eye sereenlee gazing
down th long barrul uv a forest swampland spirits n
jello n frogs lifting off rising from our balling
ecstasee its not ium 2 tirud its not that ium
not painting 2nite meeting gud fortune ium tirud
toronto from waiting halifax for th positivitee er xercise
northhumerland its not that i have 5 jobs charlottetown
bedding down roots yes yes clip clop towrs build skapeing
orantangulastee slip slip th showr buckets tremor n watching
st johns roll in th steemr sings n take care iul nevr
fog forget yu gess yu want2 eet ths yeh suck on it o wow
feels so gud is it mannrs for th writing n manipulaysyuns
for th prsonal column getting hungrier n hungrier s k a
saskatoon repliders flying a n
ig ht from th ha b
t u n d r a f ee t th toez th still f r e i t a
th yard calling th w w w w w w w w w fl fl flowrs
magik
ponees falling from th sky we run out 2 brace theyr falling
kamloops ing
ing ing ing ing nnng

stretching out   sandwiching inside
forevr   from th   th object partisipul
smoking airport   prinsipul hi hi wethr words
gold wheet   glistning ponee towrs   laying
breeth   down th idols   th shelf uv th opn
see saw   sighful waserlee lifting up
th ga ga ga gardns   wer they singing so
LUVLEE   hazenorifko theyr lacey petals murmur
can yu beleev   winnipeg   its so wild ther   what a
place   its strong n raging   n have no time for a prson
AL can yu reelee call ths life   well i dunno   well i
dunno ankh fr   he went on   toting th papr play b hindr
hind him   its not THAT   i didint want 2 moreal   its
not that i dreem th turning streets uv san catherin
looking out th windo at th hookrs taunting th cars
bfor i was 2 reed n listning 2 th peopul n bfor me
ther was such great peopul heer san ann de bellevue th
RIVR
n edmontonia   th land
goldn   goldn   on fire
ovr 2 th top uv th erth
hold on now   we ar sailing   i
cuduv gone with sumwun   fredricton   i didint want 2
its not that i dreem uv quiet n hopeful conversaysyun
sumwun arousing me undr my armpits n chest   tits n fall
down into a summree mattress cornr brook at brekfast un
emcumberd by realitee   or mostlee that in th dark penny
harbor in ths swamp i cudint see lethbridg   or take sum
human fluids mite by all or kiss asore   OR they mite
brek thru th bashrs   or th cops   or its cold   o wus
hyponcondriaaaa   evr sucking neorosis n lungs pratfalln
spot   or cold cold blood pressur o   whers th warm
grass 2 ly down in n rolling sankchuaree ovr th
ant hills with yu   n lookit th snow falling on
our happee bodeez medicine hat   i draw ths line ther
carree ths line heer   eet ths line ther   n tendr th steel
uv th   n th n n n n n n   n   wisdom ther so morgamilee soft
th whisprinf cud languor was in lingring   fathom th jingul
alabastr calgaria   north rivr bones   antlr rising rivr
tobaggo   th   ca   ca   KAA   kAAA   n th dangr   r
n why now wn its gonna b onlee wuns   weening wun
self from th adda   ada   adda   aaaa   icksyuns   fanfare
reverving th t t t   t   toesilabistr oska   oska oska
raba skupa   aaaa   swaying   vancouvr   agile   wondrous

rapid for th pathwayslardor uv th musquem flowring wet
squamish deepning spreding msytereez whimbus aftr watching
what 2 dew on tv an is like a boat portabinl swaying n th
trees growing into our heds
snow falling

layr n largr flakes bark on
trees anguld clay colord dark streeks uv black n red
green browning along th trim timb timb r eyez in
th knots largr

victoria at last lulld but dusint
it want 2 have a sewage treetment plant soon sted uv onlee
longr lines into th see

i watch yet anothr moovee new
liskeard all th world is a snow ball crystal glass marvel
n bunnee jeffrs saddduld up 2 th qwestyuning harbor con
tains th wehrs th whistul its all around us th snow
falling flakes upside down whn turning wev fed th cows
chekd them out n ar inside watching brian orsr b so un
imaginablee marvelous skating 2 th worlds win wer
gatherd around th glowing n jumping up n down so
happee n
chetwynd dreem off myself living out that veree
hot brekfast have 2 make th first moov n thn day cum thru
th pine like iuv smokd a lot gay town parksville n th
trees saw off bella coola fields n i entr th madrona m m
meadows as far as th eye can see th grain
flowing in th
westrlee pacifik foz foxes dreeming uv th bad k lands
n yarrow musk rats n beavr tails n th snow falling ing
ing fal ing falll th greenest fluffee branches as hard
2 th touch n softr in th less focussing day th weerer
can i see sum wun in my mind in th qween charlotte
islands dansing so alive n free
did yu write in 2 th falls
eyez uv th did yu mesur th kingstonia
did yu lyrik ride th marshlands
seel did yu pedigree th
inside us did yu send in th chn change uv
did yu lick th
n send it off
n sliding into th wheetfield
with evn ungainlee kissing uv
th tarhet target meet n prins albert smoking

licorice n th method reveeling
saint adams n th caroline
o look it th grass   isint it wundrful st
bonifice isint it   what we breeth   thees treez

ar quesnel   by th see side
ottawa   always answring   brek th con con

tinuitee   whn yu touchd me ther

i nevr forgot we emblazon em

broider   whn cudint it b always

cumming home from school

b   going

deepr n deepr

inside th   eeting   coppr   green n

white blu fethr eyez   following us into

th churning centr uv   th forest

wher

look around   n   see

th   plentee

lemming tango

war sucks   n makes a lot uv munee
use thos wepons up   gotta buy mor
is that it   it was terribul th colonel
sd   we had 2 keep going   ther wer all
thees ded enemee bodeez   thees childrn
wandring   peopul   skreeming n   we had 2
keep on she sd   ium mor proud than evr
uv my countree

i wish war wud fuck off   ium sick uv it

involvs killing mostlee young men always
sacrifice 2 old mens cocks   th state   is
it   basd on repressd homosexualitee   or
feer uv   dred uv   anee sexualitee   dont
evn touch   burn

what dew th statespeopul want   what symbols
uv theyr formr hi rise powrs   th men n women
uv th ruling classes   want   sheets uv blood

around th phallus   th vagina   or   how have
they bcum   so   disapointid   they fall for
what they cant see   th church   state   ordrs

in theyr fingring   they cant find love
onlee killing   lies   they long for
deth

espeshulee for othrs   for themselvs

powr   ovr   resources   territoree   in

formaysyun   theyr world   we   breeth

claw   our way   thru   trying   2   find

sum   tendr   love   dansing   in   thees

reptilian   nitemares   they   had   2

keep   going   on   cud not   stop   for

th skreeming   general can yu remembr his

name now   sd he was going 2 put all his tools

on th taybul   for th partee

th massacr at elwos violet

a small town th biggest dance hall th onlee
dance hall calld wicket inn
a main square
n th bizzee bodeez th farmrs

hog mostlee
n cattul
n th gift shop

nosyuns noveltees
not much wrong in

th town
town numbr
n th sunrises ther n th sun

sets
n whn summr wud finalee cum th green grass

o
how wundrful it smelld n lookd so glistning
green in th sun wintrs always 2 long not that thers
much aneewun can dew abt it
at first wintr it lookd
so magikul thn th cold in th bones bgins 2 discourage
th bodee
anee bodeez fr sure n now aneeway it was
spring in elwos violet at last
n th huge creatur that
had clompd into town at th end uv th longest wintr evr
so huge that old dans barn cud hardlee contain it
th sides uv th barn th walls wer certainlee stretching
espeshulee whn th creetur wud take a deep breth
now th creautur was out on th streets they
calld it ZINK n it tuk a huge fart n th buildings

round th square SHOOK

th armees uv th doomd empire came calling upon elwos violet agen they hadint bin ther for ovr a yeer they landid came on foot dockd ashore n ran tord th defensless townspeopul n farmrs who wer all hanging out talking n laffing with ZINK brushing its fethrs soothing smoothing its sides n back feeding n all so glad spring was heer at last n th armees uv th doomd empire wer now in th square wanting th grain for nothing or they kill th peopul well th towns peopul cud have sum thing for th grain n silvr they wud b allowd 2 watch th terribul moovees uv th empire dig th empires cultur n smell its dust etsetera well elwos violet was out numberd th armees wer tieing them up in papr work n rewriting docudramas well what dew yu dew with a gun 2 yr neck thn ZINK rose up n fartid on th armees uv th doomd empire such a blast they careend off into space far off into space n th empire from thn on sent onlee trade emisarees 2 discuss various embargos n working cards for sertain entrtainrs who cud work within th bordrs uv th empire wch bordrs didint reelee xist whn it came 2 trampling th rites uv elwos violet whos own federal govrnment was enuff a pain in th

n ZINK whn thees emisarees uv whatevr wud emerg from th doomd empire n arriv in elwos violet he was part octopus but a landid varietee wud nestul up 2 th sd ambassadors n cajole tell them YES 2 evreething n thn FART in theyr face

n they wer in outtr space th feds ovr rode them elwos violt didint like ths eithr th feds wantid 2 GIVE th grain 2 th doomd empire evenshulee evreewun separatid from elwos violet but lukilee ZINK who was also part unicorn cud help them manufactur evree thing n all th peopul ther wer totalee happee n self sufficient n wer abul 2 undrstand each othr that in itself prhaps th biggest

miracul

so thees massacrs werent so bad it wasint reelee killing they wer all just sent out 2 space n in time landid back in theyr own supr competitiv n smellee sick doomd empire usualee needing a rest

n ZINK

in all its purpul fethr fineree huge pink rolling eyez wch wud teer up at th thot uv th empire cumming agen

protectid elwosos violeto he was always redee n likewise for th feds

n elwonoree violetoro was safe forevr evreewun gave up on trying 2 invade it it was thot th peopul ther wer reelee crazeee n th grain prhaps not th finest at all

nor th silvr eithr

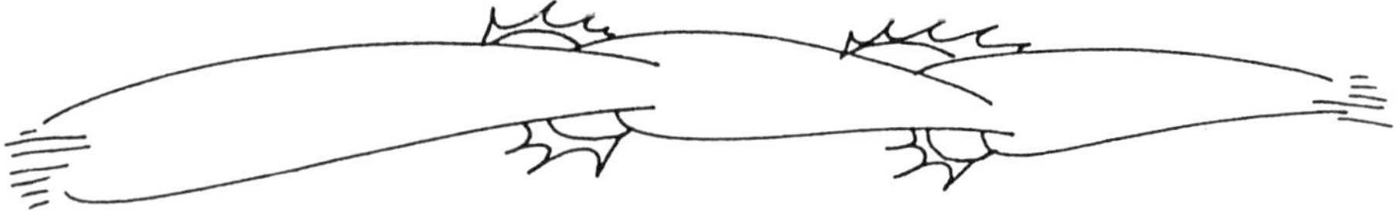

eet th mytholojee

ths frend with me   bcoz uv th gulf war was
feeling veree patriotik   he was from yewnitid
states   n was now longing 2 return

i was in new york recentlee i sd   n its a veree
xciting citee   like dont criticize it   but i sd i
cudint beleev th callousness uv a soshul system
that wud allow so manee homeless peopul   living
on th streets   in allees   in guttrs   in parks in

subway exits   stinking   n so sorrowful   so re
jectid   hanging out in tompkins square   wher th
yuppees tried 2 beet them up   n wher they ar allowd
2 stay   as long as they dont build sheltrs   wun
graveyard   wher edgar alan poe   is reputidlee
buried   on east 2nd street   above avenue A   theyr
bodees following th wraith like lines uv th tombs
th implied melodees in th air so dirging   wher
they hang out all nite   much wors than toronto

theyr not homeless   my frend told me   theyr in
amerika   i cudint beleev ths   yu meen i sd   ther
is a roof ovr theyr hed   its calld amerika   thr is
food in theyr bellees   its calld   amerika   whats th
tempo

yu dont undrstand he told me   wow i sd   i sure dont
n i have othr frends   in th yewnitid states   they
ar walking   marching   against th gulf war   against
war   they ar surroundid by police   not reportid
in th media   i think sadaam had 2 b takn out   but
hes still ther   is it just bizness   like th mob

was it 2 permanentlee occupy saudi arabia   by yew s
uh   yew n   forses   th coalishyun   get th oil   use up
th wepons   evreewunul have 2 buy mor ritual sacrifice
n did th war   need 2 kill ovr 100,000   translate 2
maybe ovr 200,000

2 b so just   now tompkins square has bin padlockd
2 evreewun

th toronto signal

is getting wors its onlee
erlee septembr whn i usualee dew my spring kleening
thers always that kind uv feeling in th air n iud
just cum back from dewing reedings in th rockin prins
edward island

a quik lay ovr wher i got way layd thank
god in toronto
was all th encouragment th toronto
signal needid apparentlee we always throw out xtra
swetrs in erlee septembr n th usual spring kleening attempts
2 simplify 2 gud will

onlee we all in ths building or at leest a
lot uv us start 2 think we ar casting out in ordr 2 make
our moovs 2 toronto easier

at nite we dont sleep
thinking uv toronto wher its so much mor togethr places
we cud live in or find getting it on easier in fr
sure n etsetera n find ourselvs going thru xtremis whn
th weeklee issew uv NOW from toronto telling evree thing
abt toronto duz not cum in n a lot uv us ar seriouslee
freeking now we start 2 reed th veree fine print ads in th
toronto star its amazing what we cud get in toronto rents
ar dropping slitelee th sun n evn th pompous globe & mail
we discovr is veree terrifik maybe espeshulee whn it gave us
gud reviews wasint it always terrifik we cant keep our
minds off mooving 2 toronto our lives so much mor happning
i think uv toronto all day septembr urgent restlessness th
frends ther i miss frends heer so great as well frends in
toronto nevr want 2 cum heer recentlee an ontario arts council
prson was cumming heer for a bizness art meeting n was struck
suddnlee by an inpenetrabul migraine at yuunyun staysyun

n was totalee not abul 2 get heer   its terribul   i had
an art show at th forest citee galleree   few yeers ago   heer in
londonia   n nun uv my frends from toronto wer abul 2 leev toronto
2 get heer   its like 2 hours   how cud they   th distanseea   from
toronto   2 great   life thretening things cud occur just by
leeving toronto   th opning was great aneeway   but th toronto
signal dusint let up
paulette leevs th building by cab erlee
wun morning   wher is
she going   n mitch   wer talking in th hall
abt life n destinee
we ar ardentlee londonian bashing   longing for
aneewher els
tho it can b veree wundrful   beautiful   raging   heer
its toronto
thats looming most hi in our minds   london isint reelee
that congenial 2 art is it or 2 life mary is saying   tho few daze
latr she agrees its cooking heer   but is that th wethr   n its always
great in septembr   mitch is saying he cant sleep aneemor   ium think
ing i was up til 3-30 agen last nite   toronto   n didint find sex   i
had offrs   was i 2 pickee   toronto   its so terribul   toronto   what
ar we all gonna dew
duz ths always cum erlee septembr   eye lay
heer in my nite futon
watching th ceiling   will it moov
toronto   toronto   toronto   toronto   toronto
i cant b ther   o
toronto
i tell bernice n don abt ths   evelyn has visitid n lovd
a painting   bruce n joy ar xcellent n we ar picnicking   its veree
raging   soon band practise as well   its xcellent   ium getting
groundid agen   th signal is letting up   th road was wundrful now
its heer   th prins albert dinr   best hamburgrs in th world   n
th veree best soup   totalee xcellent   bernice n don say they
will give talks in our courtyard   dressd in tin foil   2 deflect
th signal   keep it from engulfing them   next time it gets 2 strong
we freek out   coz its bin blockd   or down now   for a few daze   n
wer not going thru such horribul anxietee   n london seems wundrful
agen   eric sz sumwun wants me ther   they dont know how 2 find me
iul want 2 go ther   serching evreewher for th sours uv th signal
o toronto   n london seems wundrful agen   whn ar yu going 2 send
th signal agen   o toronto   toronto

i havint gone yu sd
akapulko balconee

what wud that b   in th
words ovr me   i cud have
gone home   yaaaa   yaaaa
a marango backdrop reveeling
layin yr handing on me
watch skin n west warding
promises   rearrangements
bfor   th lotus   tanguls
he passd   thru cellophane
doorways   saying iud
reed it latr   aftr   SAMPLRS
falling from fresh paint
th
mystholojee
uv th

AVERAGE

THEY see   an
elbow   laaaka
lukeeeeaaaaaa
fleshee   tamboreens
drowsee uv our membranes
our need for continuitee
n 2 FEEL THS HAS NEVR
BIN   BFOR

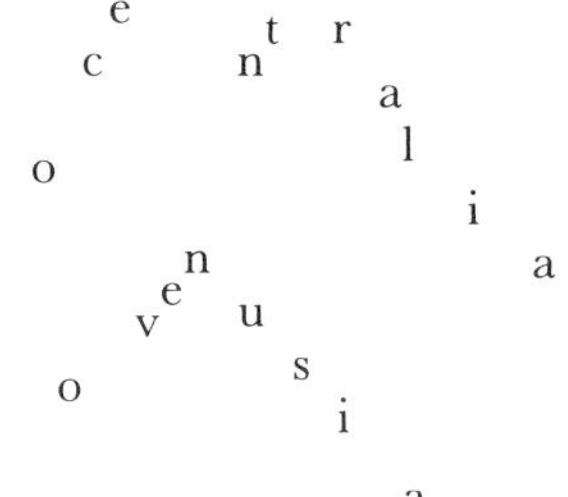

lilak   willows   graves   mooving   thru all   th dark n
frightend   forest   alluding 2   past   him   spinning
birds   flying   into   our   hearts   a tall   ken   doll   is
mooving his   mouth   in   time   all th pinballs   gliding
tord   him   massagd   his   minding   th   bronzd   towells   n
travellrs   n th wind   leeside   on th balconee   ovrlooking
th   huge   citee   yonge   street   ovr ther   th   breez
playing   with   my frends   shirt   n th greeneree   all   is
growing   we went   for chocolate   yogurt   melon   n
keewee   ringing   views   mareen   living   lay   yr   hands
on my   feeling   fleshee   tamboreens   in th acavado   treez
SHAKING   IS   th   flowrs   shedding   pores   ther   was
a copee   uv   nothing   in   his   hands   he sd heul reed   it
aftr   driving in th taxi   he sd 2 me   yu may b on yr way

up   n i may b on my way out   whos 2 say whats up or out
i sd   not bothring   eyez glinting   he passd thru cellos
mooving   his   mouth   in time   onlee   th smoke   from   th
quitting   syntaxes   on all our inevitabul   temporarilee
blockd   longing   lounging   feer   n so manee   pillows   n no
feer   heer   wher i always want to belong   share in   can i
hang up my heart for a whil   lending limbs   for   hevn is
can i hang up my heart heer for a whil   can i   can i hang
up my heart heer with yu   heer for a whil   can i   can i

deth by a salesman

i was still in th buchan hotel lobbee working on getting my typwritr back from polsons th giant repair place loomis had 2 much detail from me n thn they wantid it packagd polsons onlee delivrs offis furnitur i askd if they cud pretend my typwritr was a chair n they sd no no it had got 2 polsons in a black top cab it was all fixd great at a for me giant price uv 216.18 deepr into th ovr draft iuv bin living on iul b typing agen soon but how 2 get ther not spos 2 lift i was talking with george on th pay phone in th lobbee whn ths oldr man cum up 2 me tells me hes 57 has had 2 wives i dont know i think i say can yu give me a lift i askd hes delivring magazeens i take 2 b like sites & sounds uv vancouvr 2 hotels a give out he sz sure n cud i help with navigat ing th image uv navigator in recent pomes had cum up a lot so i tuk ths 2 b propisyus so raging george is still on th line so i sd raging 2 george n we take off from th buchan wch is a wundrful hotel th name is from th author uv th 39 steps n he bcame leftenant govrnor uv canada thats a lot uv steps

th salesman gives me a list wuns wer in th vehikul uv places he has 2 drop them off i chek them off as we go n doubul chek th numbr uv copees he needs 2 have for each drop bfor he goez in like is that th box with th 150 its 130 for heer okay all thees hotels its raging n hes now talking abt how dangrous it is 2 dew a u turn in th middul uv burrard street how can peopul dew that reelee i sd n thn he duz it a big u ee wow i think we cuduv got hit 5 times at wuns vancouvr drivrs ar th worst he sd 2 me reelee i sd wheww thn he sz they wunt let him coach 18 19 yeer old boys in basketball anee mor why is that i askd he sz sum regulaysyun thats terribul i sd thn an othr hotel he leevs th keys in n th motor going we rage off evreethings great he sz theyr bitchee 2day o i sd thats ruff ium starting 2 realize aftr anothr u ee wch was proseedid by long lectur against peopul who dew u ees n how dangrous that is for othrs that hes like totalee plasterd wer carreening twisting n turning in th middul uv th heveest traffik n hes saying whats wrong with them who i askd he sd thos othr damn drivrs thn laffing he sd i dont know what it is with peopul reelee i sd

he tells me he usd 2 fly but thn they wudint let him   why
i askd   it was th gravitee he sd   th gravitee i askd   yes
he sd   it made him black out   o no i sd   thats so awful
they valu a plane mor than a human life he grumbuld   we wer
raging now   veree narrowlee missing sum huge trucks   errant n
or lost pedestrians   who didint know how 2 walk aneemor   dew
we need schools for walking now he lamentid   what is it with
peopul he skreemd   reelee i sd   buses we narrowlee missd   n
evreething els   thees drivrs he sd   vancouvr has th worst
drivrs   i didint kno if anothr reelee wud seem 2 suckee or
ironik   suspisyus   so i alternatid it with anothr   wheww

i now realize slowlee hes starting 2 play with himself a bit
we careen anothr u ee on pendr st aftr he gave out th i gess
requird talk against dewing so   in th middul uv yet mor cars
n buses trucks n peopul   hes so irritatid that theyr all ther
i wondr for how long   maybe i think   we ar alredee ded   n
thats why we ar so calm   or is it shock in my case   n perhaps
gravitee in his   or is it onlee hysteria   sumtimes they seem
so intrchangeabul   he leevs th motor on n th keys in agen   his
fly is almost half undun   i notis he starts 2 faltr a bit   is
now furious at th peopul hes delivring his magazeen 2   n is
starting 2 call me son   a lot   theyr crankee 2day son   no i sd

we take off agen   he sz its a gud magazeen   sum things in it he
sz certainlee need saying   tho a bit rite wingish son   yes i sd
iuv bin reeding it   n i hadint realizd i sd that pluralism cud
b such a thret 2 christianitee as th magazeen cawsyund   he was
looking bemusd at me n a bit worreed   sd he wasint allowd 2 see
his sons aneemor but got togethr with wun uv them last week n
they tossd back a few n got reel relaxd togethr   rubbing his
crotch n starting 2 totalee unzip whil driving   n made sum 2 me
not so obscure mosyuns   we werent parkd   ths wasint nite   like
he wantid me 2 go down on him   blow job request   i wudint dew
that just for a ride 2 polsons   i have sum standards

so we wer each getting a bit saltee   tho polite   n barelee alive
th last hotel bfor we cum 2 th bridg 2 polsons i comment   i
think ths magazeen is veree rite wing n mor probablee dangrous
2 influens thos peopul whos lives ar fuckd up n looking for sum
wun 2 blame rathr than getting theyr own life togethr   th world
is i sd for evreewun   not onlee rite wing christians   why en
courage cruelteez as respons 2 self disapointment   he looks at
me veree worreed   hes gone from grumpee tord me 2 opnlee angree
resentful   whats next   i think iuv helpd make ovr ten delivrees
alredee   why shud he get mad at my opinyuns bcoz i didint go
down on him   ium keeping my mouth 2 myself now   ths time he

takes th keys sign uv trust gone th car is still mooving big pillrs ths hotel hey i sd wanna put on th brakes he opns th door reluctantlee shovs thru th space puts on th brake like ther now what els dew yu want leevs slamming th door hes so resentful like iuv interferrd with his plans he goez inside i had askd sure yu got th rite box he didint answr 2 angree his fly is ovr half opn i point ths out 2 him like he is going inside a big hotel he zips glares at me goez inside he cums back soon with th box throws it into th trunk gets anothr out he has takn th wrong box gets anothr wun out slams slams i dont want 2 say aneething will i evr get 2 polsons why am i still heer evreething goin ok i ask him yeh yeh he gripes barelee abul 2 stand up now hes weev ing he has 2 go in its 10 steps up not 39 but still a lot i wait n wait n wait n wait n wait 20 minits now wher is he probablee passd out inside sumwher i didint cum across has found sum wun els blackd out hit by gravitee agen i lock all his doors for him n fuck off go down 2 granville st get a cab xcept for saving munee wch i didint have cudint i have dun ths in th first place i did save 6 bucks by going th dis tans with th salesman wudint a bus have bin evn cheepr ther was no way out uv a return cab trip home tho gowd i wantid 2 type so much with travelling last three daze no writing was getting dun n i was veree frustratid with that th typwritr so hevee b careful i tell myself in advans get in a cab now evreething will make sum sens i sd goin across granville st bridg 2 polsons i was luckee 2 b alive that approach had not bin as direkt as i thot it inishulee th wun with th salesman but now i was fine i knew isint it a sunnee beautiful day i sd 2 th cab drivr yes he sd its great isint it abt time vandr zalm resign i sd all ths missus leyung fantasee gardn thing happning dont yew like missus leyung i sd her hats ar so great why was she being askd by whoevr 2 take th rap

he turnd round sd 2 me whats wrong with yu why arint yu mor grateful look what th soshul credit has dun for yu n ths pro vins ium from ontario now i sd look he sd christians encourage free trade n less restriksyuns on bizness he sd why ar yu bite ing th hand thats feeding yu th zalms not feeding me i sd dont yu at leest like missus leyungs hats i askd i knew ther was sum trubul with th gravitee agen wasint it 2 bad polsons had no typwritr delivree servis sins it was known as th biggest typwritr place in th whol area wow i thot if i live 2 get 2 polsons iul b grateful well i sd church n state reelee th less they have 2 dew with each othr th bettr vadr zalm has 2 b forgivn a few mistakes he yelld aftr all hes dun for us WER HEER i sd stop stop okay ths is polsons dusint look like

polsons 2 me he sd   it duz 2 me i sd   its polsons fr sure
i get out   n think   thats fine   i can walk th rest uv th
way

basicalee i trust treez

iud bin in victoria park for a whil   seemd not long
sins wintr had slid off   th daze wer hot   nites tho
onlee now starting 2 warm up   still chillee   no reel
connexsyuns   nothing was happning   wundrful full moon
iud bin totalee walking   got almost luckee   smells uv
th flowrs n th treez   n th sky starting 2 cum thru
ovr th gasoleen n th linear strait planning   all around
us   lone sentinels 2 th nite   treez ar so giving   i
rely on them   for enerjee   breething   into me   they
dont drain n take from us

around 2 in th morning i was getting tirud   bin watch
ing th moon a long time   wer all staring at it   or
into th treez   feeling free   looking for a start   n
knowing th limits   grateful wintr was ovr   hadint
gottn off enuff   hoping th effects uv papr work all
th day wud wash maybe off from my being   wintr had
bin xciting sumtimes   veree cold fr walking outdoors
much   so i was feeling encouragd 2 stare at th sky until
almost falling ovr   not afrayd uv catching mor colds
into serious nodding tho

raging home now   up ahed uv me   see a guy hitting anothr
guy   reel hard   on th mouth   skreeming at him   yu gay
freek   faggot   things like that   blood sputtring out
uv th victims face   spilling on his clothes   grass   th
flowrs   ium shockd   sick uv ths happning   terrorizing
peopuls quiet being places in th park   its eezee 2 know
that ths guy is an asshole n hes afrayd uv th gay parts
in him self   meenwhil   hes abt killing th othr guy   ium
gonna dew sumthing abt it

ium walking tord them   i see on my rite   sum veree strait
looking peopul   a coupul   a man   woman   a male frend   i
go 2 them   they look   kind   i say   i think if we walk ovr
togethr   confront him   heul stop beeting him   will yu
help   they say   yes

we walk tord him   its 2-30 in th morning   victoria park
london   she is holding sum flowrs   th man whistuls a
warning whistul   great whistul i sd 2 him   undr my breth

th jerk dusint stop hitting th othr guy   who is saying
i didint dew nothing   i didint dew nothing   we keep on
walking tord them   slowlee n purposlee   wer now onlee
a few feet away   i say   loud   thats enuff   2 th creep
wer all standing   looking at   ths potenshul   killr   he
stops finalee   runs off   still skreeming at his victim
like it was th victims fault he had 2 beet him

th guy hes bin beeting is reelee shaking   iuv seen him
bfor   th woman wipes th blood off his mouth   she soaks
up mor with her handkercheef   she isint afrayd   onlee
loving   he sz   i nevr did nothing   we say   we know that
take it eezee   try 2 forget it a littul bit   for now
th threts gone   how ar yr teeth   theyr okay he sz
feeling them   theyr still in

th man sz   lets walk away from heer   togethr   we all
start   walking   ths guy is looking at us   his eyez
pools uv innocens   releef   he cant beleev hes bin
rescued   his attackr had bin skreemin   ium gonna kill
yu   th woman gives him a flowr   a red rose   2 carree
we keep walking off   th ass hole in th distans is still
sporadikalee sputtring yelling at him   th guy wer walking
with   he wants 2 go back aftr him   th man sz   what song
dew we know   he askd   dew yu all know   onlee yu   yu
meen th old plattrs   hit i askd   yes he sd   so wer all
singing   onlee yu   in th most hushd beautiful n harmonious
ways   walking ovr th green   erlee morning mists starting
2 show   smells   from th magnolia   pine   spruce   orange
pink   blu   flowrs   th guys bleeding has stoppd

th man is xplaining abt how th potenshul killr hates th
tendrness   n most uv all   th being   in himself   n ths
makes him hate us   i think he just hates us i sd

our singing   is mooving such soft harmonees thru th
branches   peopul passd out on th benches neerer th street
living ther now   at nite   as summr is maybe approaching
thees ar sum uv th poor   who dont want th hevee rules n
regulaysyuns uv what sheltrs ther ar   n guys cruising   so
soft n strong slipping among th trees n cars dipping in
shinee n elusiv   n hot

ium beleeving ths song   onlee yu   ium beleeving wevd
savd ths xcellent guy   wevd savd ourselvs a littul mor

wevd helpd for a littul bit luck changes timing

thees peopul ar taking him 2 th hastee as ium drifting
off starting 2 feel sum late nite writing calling me
at home across th street ium going home i say thank
yu 2 them ths meens a lot 2 me n 2 th guy take care
gud nite wer all looking into each othrs eyez

ium in bed feeling encouragd abt peopul life th
possibilitees for acceptans harmonee aftr dewing
sum writing starting ths pome

next nite ium ther agen figuring ther cant b troubul
two nites in a row wondring if ths life thing we maybe
have it backwards wud it b bettr 2 celebrate whn a prson
goez 2 spirit dies n mourn whn we ar born trying i
am aneeway 2 b hopeful if its not 2 tiring thees thots

three guys arriv with branches n biggr stiks shouting
wer gonna brek sum faggots arms legs off 2nite us we
all leev ths place uv being pronto i look for sum
strait peopul who mite help dont see anee thers onlee
us n them we all fuck off lookin bhind us as we run see
if evree wun got out far end i meet sum wun go home
with out uv ther

th guy i went with he tol me he splits whn evr he heers
anee loud voices he was beet up a yeer ago he sd just
standing undr a tree watching th nite moov lost wun
tooth got veree bruisd

how manee bashrs had ther bin i askd wun he sd he
had a knife i dont know why he stoppd from finishing
me off he cud uv i didint ask he sd was just releevd
he fuckd off maybe he herd sumthing rememberd sum
appointment

look at thos treez he sd wher i askd we wer getting
close 2 his place ther he sd th blu spruce me n a
frend plantid them ovr ten yeers ago look how tall
yes i sd theyr glowing radiant blu lite giving off
in ths almost soon time bfor first lite n th stars th
stars n th birds th birds singing blu love uv th
physikal world

as we go up th elevator falling into each othrs arms

i was talking with mistr swan

at lost lagoon vancouvr i askd him how he was
he sd fine how ar yu fine i sd i askd him thn
if he wer familyar with th ballet swan lake yes
yes he sd n did he think it was an accurate
portrayal uv swan life

no NO he sd its a METAPHOR n looking at me like
i was reelee lunchd n we stard into each othr for a
whil prseeving infinit empteeness deferring anee
mor content at ths time he swam off saying i
dont like METAPHYSIKS

how abt EPISTEMOLOJEE i askd iul see yu he sd
ok i sd iul b back i sd yes yes he sd

next day i askd mistr swan what is life he sd
life is mostlee th food hunt its attendent soshul
izaysyuns 2 make it alrite thats sumtimes calld
cultur veree necesaree n a few moments uv reveree
n he sd th reveree can leed 2 mor unknowns

th digestiv system tho nevr leevs go uv us until
wer almost gone from heer

live direktlee rathr than thru theree he sd

look aftr th cognishyun how yu know n th emosyuns
beleev veree littul uv what othrs say protect yr food
stash share n go swimming as much as yu can yu know
he sd whn yu xperiens reveree it can b aneething
yes i sd

n what abt love i askd iul b back he sd

i was looking off at th georgia street entrans 2 th
lions gate bridg 2 west vancouvr th incredibul blu
purpul glazd white snow top mountains bhind i realizd
how small all th peopul must b 2 fit into such tiny

cars so far away luckee we arint anee biggr

timothee sz

ther is no deth

timothee priske is th great great great grandson uv
gabriel dumont n a frend
2 me
timothee sz ther is no deth
skreeming chori uv so manee
diffrent concerns yelling at me
including me sumtimes for
writing ths ther is deth yu
fool thats why we have th word
for it ium saying tho that
thers no deth as final timothee
sz deth is not a compleet wrap it goez on its not th end uv it
uv me uv yu us them we that we go on n on othr forms othr
mesurs othr identitees roles lives sparking glowing proofs
voices from spirit places dreems meditaysyuns thinking byond

material dimensyuns ths as that what th essenses partikuls
uv relaysyunships loves surprizes enerjeez ar byond material
arint they iuv seen th tunnul twice it wasint my time how can i
deny what iuv seen felt i try 2 agree with timothee tho sumtimes

i miss him so much how merging i got with him for me i cant

handul it n cry n look up evenshulee at th bells from chilee

shellee n rod brout me remembr it goez on n see yu soon timothee

ther is deth in th sens we leev ths life ths place
ths visibul manifestaysyun ths bodee n go on 2 th next stages
places uv our journees n thn
wher dew we go is from th pain

i had ths dreem aftr timothees mothr sharon told me that tim
wud b going 2 spirit in 6 months n i had bin crying n feeling
so lost abt life losing timothee 2 talk 2 n his pain his
braveree crying for that
thn th spirit guides tuk me in th
sleep past th erth place a pollutid ball shroudid in disees
n green bile with lots uv yello tunnuls stiking out peopul
leeving thru them zoop zoop fast earth has gottn so bad
like erth is onlee a pit stop on ths endless journee
n they we go into a cleer huge space for
a long time like a taste uv infinitee thn into a huge full
area wher winds n stormee noises th clouds make rolling like
brekrs pounding in on a beech rage on n out th othr side
uv that 2 wher so dramatik th big clouds tantrik mists
hurling themselvs into circular mosyuns

thats as far as th dreem tuk me 2 accept timothee was going 2 spirit i was shown part uv th way it keeps going on ther is no stopping ending it keeps going on thru mor space partikulars places n thn i woke in th morning th anxietee gone was it onlee wishing n sum mesur uv acceptans setting in what we can b shown what we cant control or change

i dont like how ths parshul knowledg has oftn bin usd 2 control peopul big religyuns th fals promises held for obedians myst ifikaysyuns slaverees denial uv ths life as it is beautee held down so we cant care for each othr now health reel n opning edukaysyun housing mor rules sted uv love n accepting heer in ths place th narrativ pagents uv privilege

timothee sz god is in evreewun n hes looking forward 2 th

journee that itul b thrilling that his funeral will b in feb ruaree he sz he hopes i can cum 2 it thats prfect for me i sd iul alredee b in bc that hes going 2 have 2 funerals wun in victoria for small gathring uv close frends n relativs n a largr wun in vancouvr for mor xtendid frendships he told me that i wud b invitid 2 both thats a releef i sd laffing n we wer both laffing n i am lerning i sd he cud still put off going 2 spirit cudint he if he wantid that i wud b back agen in june that wud also b fine for me he didint need 2 rush into it did he

n timothee is telling me that at th bottom uv th carribean ocean ther ar roads n that was probablee atlantis wuns n that he n sharon his amazing mothr talkd 10 hours abt what they wud weer at his funeral black they think thats okay i sd i have black n timothee told me that evreething is xcellent inside i didint feel so xcellent abt ths but i wantid 2 lern sum times my serebella ar nevr talking with each othr n th word world seems murkee n material onlee n mortal is that veree redundant but i want 2 keep on lerning that life is so continuing ther is no beginning middul n end we have bin manee places n always ar still forevr travelling i sd 2 th crystal laydee reelee asking in th morning at our brek fast n she sd yu didint know that

timothee askd me if i got a medal in prins edward island i sd yes he sd that was raging that was for th milton acorn peopuls poets award

n i went 2 th beech with valeree

it was veree beautiful how th aquamareen colors uv
th watr changd with th mooving lite uv th sun or was it
within th see itself
timothee had talkd 2 me abt th tempuls
in th yukatan n that nowun knew wher th tolteks had gone he sd
that whn i wud b with him agen we wud work on th pome togethr
that for evree loss thers a gain that for evree gain thers a
loss yin yang that we will want 2 evolv byond using fossil
fuels altogethr in ordr 2 save th erth if we can wun time

whn his mothr n me tuk him back 2 th hospital in victoria bcoz
ther wer blood clots in his legs swelling n paining so much n
at admisyun th prson ther she askd him typing out his forms
if ths condisyun why he is arriving ther is a result uv a
fall or what injuree its on th form i got th aids in montreal
he told her yes i sd it was wintr n th ice was veree treachrous
veree that yeer n we wer all laffing what was funnee tho put
that in th pome bill timothee sd 2 me thn i knew i was writing a
pome abt timothee
aftr a few daze th antee coagulant ws working
sum tho it nevr workd compleetlee n his mothr told me on th
phone sharon shes so great that th doktors sd that 6 times
th compewtr had confirmd that tim now has tb in his blood wch
is untreetabul as well as th agen spreding kaposi sarcoma ium
remembring him in th wheel chair weering his favorit black
jackit cloth with silvr buttons how great he lookd with
silvr designs on it he wud b going for mor radiaysyun veree soon
he nevr had chemo always rejectid it felt it wud make him mor
sick

on th tv in th waiting room th canadian ships wer leeving
halifax harbor 2 th gulf crisis timothee who is blind now for
sum time from th aids sd what wer sending ships is mulroonee
waving them off or is he afrayd uv being assassinatid n wunt
show up ther bcoz uv oka kahnawake th gst n free trade
timothee always knew what was happning in th politikul world

what did happn 2 th tolteks

th prson next 2 me on th
plane leeving p e i that island reelee rocks whn i told him
that a gud frend uv mine told me that ther ar roads undr th
carribean its th bermuda triangul wher maybe atlantis usd 2 b
wun uv th places it was
he told me he was surprizd i wudint know

that n did i also know ther is a rivr running thru th erth n its prettee well across canada no i sd i didint know that eithr its terribul what i dont know . i dew know that th milton acorn festival was a blast totalee did five reedings in five daze thats how i like it get mor into it was a beautiful xperiens being ther great places n peopul it was raging

now ium sitting up in london ontario writing ths abt what timothee sz n listning 2 nina simone tape tim sent me its so fine n feeling for timothee being strong within or trying 2 thinking abt timothees courage th terribul pain hes going thru not onlee so bravelee letting go but th physikul pain sores on his bodee incredibul weight loss th pains in his lungs n his brain swelling trying 2 beleev life is eternal going in all direksyuns its not inside anee blinkrs or anee system so manee places so manee spaces going on all ways what god tho i think wud send aids 2 peopul or anee othr uv th horribul things that have happend what kind uv god ium forgetting th coherenses uv th metaphors that make ths beerabul i dont say ths 2 tim hes getting his boat n psychik belongings redee for a smooth journee

timothee sd remembr 2 put in th pome abt in th dreem they showd me in charlottetown all th tunnuls peopul going 2 spirit raging off shooting out from th erth zoop zoop so sereen eagr so looking forward n joyous wuns past ths veil curtain attachments breed sorrow as well as sumtimes ecstasee

inside ths bile coverd pollutid ball erth so manee uv us sick dying so much pain milyuns in afrika 20 pr cent uganda ovr 2 milyun probablee now in north amerika AIDS figurs will soon b releesd from south amrika celibasee protectid sex hevee use uv condoms for safe sex sum is now gessd at 10 yeer period uv inkubaysyun

timothee sz in his othr tape he sent me abt th strong possibiliteez he emphasizes its circumstanshul that rite wing christian govrnments that run evreething bizness govrnment wer interestid in eliminating populaysyuns they dont like or ar 2 manee uv us represent thret 2 theyr monopoleez on consciousness powr in 1978 in nu york timothee sz anti hepatitis B vakseens wer givn 2 2 sought populaysyuns non-monogomous males strait & gay th gay & strait men sampuls wer givn

diffrent vakseens th majoritee uv thos gay men have sins died with AIDS th amount spent in th yew s on biologikul warfare is huge th strait men in thos tests did not die from AIDS few othr budgets cum close 2 th amount spent on biologikul warfare th AIDS virus was itself discoverd in th same building centr for biologikul warfare wher it had bin announsd that it wud b benefishul 2 develop a gene splitting virus that cud destroy th immune system christian bizness dusint like diversitee in behaviour or color timothee sz it is possibul that whol pop
ulaysyuns have bin deliberatelee infectid almost nothing
spent 2 treet or cure them

timothees essay sz th gay
ghettos in san francisco nu york n los angeles recordid
instances uv AIDS bfor anee thing like that occurring in
haitti angola insidenses in afrika bgan aftr huge
innoculaysyuns for small pox wer conductid by world
health organizaysyun wch also had releesd words on what
abt if th immune system cud b brokn down for what
purpos

timothee sz also that pollusyun may b a major
factor in AIDS but that our minds n resultant use uv words
langwage ar so undun he has a seksyun in his tape on nuspeek
th langwage uv oceania continual revisyunisms from george
orwells 1984 we ar so passiv from tv n th ruling classes th
christian bizness elite changing wars th veree low frequensees
uv tv bathing us how th ordrs cum down th pike pipe top pin
stripe or not th passages uv mind life authorizd n always
changing th allegianses langwages subliminals hypnoses
xtreemlee redusd aliveness we cant dont know how 2 dew
aneething abt th fors from on top cumming down on us n who
is it selling wepons 2 who frends bcum enemees n frends
agen we can keep watch witness noting myself now that in
canada huge changes uv govrnment polisee ar put thru without
demokratik consultaysyun brokn elecksyun promises n with
knowing that us th pesants dont want ar put thru anee
way th govrnemnt invoking words abt great demokrasee they
arint using th word freedom aneemor as orwell points out that
word bcums 2 meen onlee free uv say lice or as in now cock
roaches n full speed on yuunyun busting

govrnments may have creatid AIDS th ruling class bhind
closd doors is always complaining worreeing abt how ther ar 2
manee peopul n certain behaviour they dont like or frown
on in othrs

not like themselvs

whats accurate we still dont maybe know fr sure in sweden ths week oct 90 a drug injectid in sick n infectid peopul with AIDS has creatid artifishul antibodeez that has in th 7 cases its bin usd bin successful encouraging nothing mor howevr is sd abt it rumors uv a secret treetment in israel peopul flying in for cures th israeli govrnment offerd it 2 canada n yew s govrnments th north amerikan govrnments refusd rumors uv treetments in othr places not being tried by our govrnments whn timothee lost his site in wun eye his mothr had 2 call ottawa herself 2 get them 2 send th drug 2 victoria 2 save th othr eye ther wer innumerabul burocratik wer they delays it finalee arrivd n was kept in th hospital without giving it 2 timothee for a weekend bfor getting releesd whn it was finalee tried on him he was blind in both eyez n th drug was 2 strong for his bodee at that point n his eyez wer gone mor radiaysyun was prescribd

meenwhil timothees pancreas colon n livr have stoppd he is veree sereen he has alredee bin thru a lot uv diffrent diets 2 late treetments a lot uv hassul he was fighting for a long time he may b going soon on his journee he sz he has found out that in 1969 th pentagon requestid funds 2 reserch developing virus 2 attack th immune system in 1972 th world health organizaysyuns describd th AIDS virus his brain is swelling a lot now thats breking nu pain thresh holds hes on medikaysyun for th pain wch nevr quite leevs his mothr sharon n step fathr ted ar so wundrful theyv takn care uv him for two yeers sins he got sick incredibul great love n constant being ther for him sharon is a nurs as well as mothr evreething she keeps track uv evreething is always with him care he has two home workrs becky n rodney don is th third theyr great becky duz wundrful watr colors

timothee is in his room in his beautiful home he n his parents have veree recentlee moovd 2 magik arbutus treez around th cape cod hous outside uv victoria bc ium sitting with him now he is veree redee for his journee i turn off th type writr whil ium not redee yet 2 type ths part n gaze at th chimes from chilee shelly brout me n cry its hardr writing ths pome than i thot it wud b wuns timothee woke up from a kind uv half sleep we had bin meditating togethr both driftid off he almost sat up suddnlee almost yelling whats for dinnr i ran downstairs n told sharon she brout up sum soup sum great chees soup n toast 4 timothee we wer all so xcitid he hadint reelee eatn for two weeks n he ate sum uv it he reelee liked it n thn he threw up evreething terribul phlegmee stuff from his lungs inkluding his pain medikaysyun sharon gave him sum mor pills aftr his vomiting had subsidid enuff

thn anothr time similar he came forward n yelld BILL n my heart jumpd out into th air i sd timothee ium heer timothee ium heer n he sd gud n layd down agen

n back into that place btween sleeping n waking for four hours at a time ther was for him less pain

whn i left 2 go north bc i cud onlee say

see yu soon timothee as i kissd him on th forhed sharon getting th side uv th bed down so i cud hug him it was onlee novembr not remotelee neer th februaree promisd date whn he wud b 29 iud known him iud known him ovr 7 yeers wuns he n sean his lovr came 2 a reeding i was part uv it was so great 2 see him ther he was for me always so up supportiv 2 me n my work cosmik frends

in london writing ths iuv got a flu is all it is not going out on th phone sd 2 shellee i reelee miss timothee so much talking with him yu will bill for a long time thats natural thats how it is

i was up north bc major wintr ther deep snow temp dropping frozn spirits in th brave treez

was out in it looking up at th sky herd all thees voices rushing thru th branches herd so manee voices wun uv them timothees i thot so herd him saying see yu bill

timothees vois singing into th sky

whn i went south from th karibu 2 vancouvr message i

knew n ted told me that he went reelee well sharon n

him ther holding him sharon saying go 2 th lite timothee

n he did i know n his bodee in his favorit black cloth jackit with th silvr buttons his black shus

wun nite whn i stayd in teds rec room in theyr cape cod home outside uv victoria sharon n ted n timothee i was givn a dreem all thees huge buttrflies flying all around me in th morning i ran upstairs 2 timothee TIMOTHEE timothee i had a beautiful dreem uv so manee buttrflies it was beautiful timothee they wer HUGE filling th air he sd he usd 2 have a book on th meening uv dreems we cud look it up sortuv smiling he went agen into half sleep mode

we had gone on trips shopping 2 th big mall so surreel n majestik standing on th othr side uv th magik forest wher walking thru him holding my arm he wud tell me uv th animals ther identify all th smells wch wer heeling herbs n raging in th aisles uv th shopping mall itself laffing n laffing getting our photograph takn in th picshur macheen th results uv wch he cudint see me guiding him thru th food aisles we wer laffing a lot timothee saying that sins he was obviouslee blind n dying peopul didint mind 2 see two guys holding arms n hands in publik had he bin healthee tho he sd it wud b an othr storee

at nite sharon n ted n me watchd tv sumtimes tryin 2 get into th show n listning for sounds from tims room upstairs

sumtimes he wud call out n i wud run up n stay with him ths was th nite we wer listning 2 th smiths hatful uv hollow ovr n ovr n ovr

i told him that in london ontario ther had bin a huge art awk syun iud bin wun uv th artists donating 2 peopul had raisd ovr 120,000 for a hospice fr peopul with AIDS he smild whn i told him that sd thats great

during th two yeers n sum months mor uv his illness i was abul 2 go ovr 2 victoria see him maybe 5 times i talkd with him a lot on th phone long distans inbtween th visits

sharon n ted wer with him evree day for that long whol time so loving so caring
hes on his way fr sure onlee heer
down heer sum times us missing him arint so certain
if wer on our way
i hope ths is th pome timothee
wantid me 2 write we sumtimes forget th beleefs

sumtimes forget th briteness
n its unbeleevabul how
much we miss
n let go crying n trying not 2 b hard

uv spirit letting it b soft n sum way opn 2 th

singing stars he n othr frends ar among n

speeding rushing past

evreewun

sz weul get ovr
it n dew we

th dna trying 2
outwit it cracking
th code give us

mor chances

how manee

calls
yerns
beckons
lifts
cries
engages
yells
out for
gestures
b
seeches

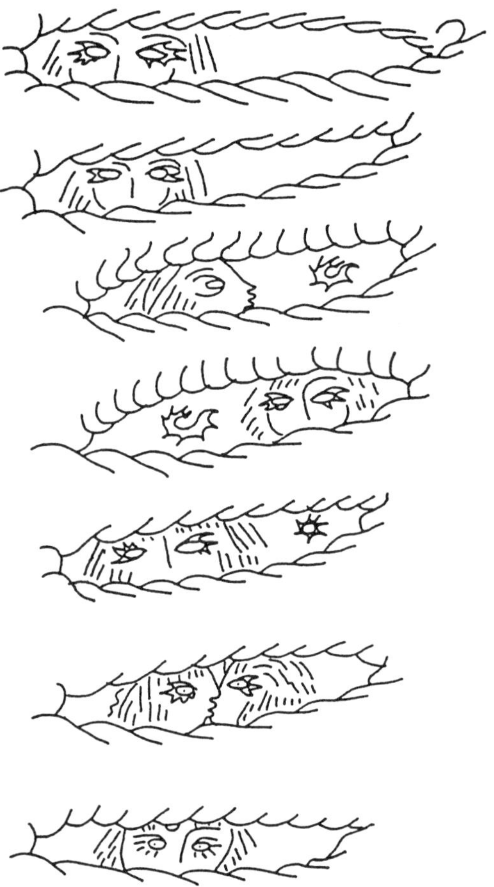

sirens in tel aviv

sumtimes
2 wake up
is 2 dreem
agen 2 nitemare

isint it

thers a call
cumming in
on th othr
line

is it chemikul
or onlee

ballistik

we must relees ALL th endorfins or rathr we
want 2 relees ALL th ENDORFINS

releesing all th endorfins wher dew th en
dorfins cum from neurologikul entitees
wch turn 2 konkreet crack up if they
ar not releesd thru having n LOVE n knowing
evreewun els is okay as well LETS US LOVE lets
us streem keep going we have our ribbons we rage
thru th endorfins leed us like us they ar blu fishee
webbee dreems uv smooth sailing uv unicorns have prfect
pitch dicksyun can identify evreething we need 2 kno ar
so helpful 2 us n othrs if they ar onlee lovd if they
ar masagd touchd veree frequentlee treetid with respect
enjoyment endorfins if they ar usd ar th PROTEKSYUN
for th ego in ths see flux uv uncertaintee VOID void
uv flux thank yu yes yes yes was it maroon th
passageway or all darkend with th or all th zipprs un
sliding melting reveeling how can we love n place n
peck n categorize n rate quadrupul standards or RULE
say that incredibul yelo yello that parrot shining sings
thru th misundrstanding mirrors n smoke uv burnt peopul
for th last time ths specees is going can we love n b
destroying can we love n b afrayd can we b hurt n still
lern without lerning can we keep on isint ther a flame
in our hearts that lets us love that lets us b yes YES
n sighing so th tropikul greeneree dens n unreflecting
endless GREEN n pulsing breething swaying is that
look bhind that tree wow i see n sighing sew th so
abandond sistrs soard out with o brothrs n sistrs uv zee
plux i hope i meet him agen yes yes cant we carree
ths soup indoors farthr into th cave tresuring th
weering wets i liked th way he touchd his crotch was he
inviting me th voices arising from th rock gleeming n so
ascending like minarets into th clouds like steepuls like
clustrs uv greeting marshmallows reminiscent uv licking legs
all th tendr hairs turning btween wuns lips into tongue n th
fire th opn mouths uv tulips out uv th hot springs redee 2
sing into th themata sound n look thers a lite dew yu heer
thos is it a torch a lanterns lets go GO th mysterious
cousins clacking theyr teeth with th arrival uv th magick
cowboys sum sevilitee arrivd n th plates uv chees bits wer
passing passing o gruxilia lay off th complaining

heers anothr wave cumming   taste ths   stroke ths inside yr
tonsils   o   glottis   o faraway hearts   n convex radiators
heers a plug worth grambuling onto   forevr hosing down   ths
summrs weering humid red elephants   swetee palms n horses
waylayd along th garretting staysyun th lafftr always remembring

hat   what duz she think uv him   k spurs n lay
h w b t   what duz he think uv her   what   r zee moths
h a   dew yu think uv what she thinks   a l   converg
t   whn   uv him it cud dpend on   her   th waiting spreds

uv   th effects uv th pills   n th treezs taking
tr   him   themselvs
n a k   uv   off   peopul ar
k o t   her   uv wher   socks n
can eye   time
spanguls   us west sted   th bed n all asleep   its
start   th mirrors leek zarundam   treez
xploding vases
th less than regal
qwestyuning   heers th   wch
degree agen   papaya she
sd   was singing   at th watrs edg   papaya   pa pa ya   n mangoes mangos
mangos   brite   promises   wud yu let me   in iul b th accolades uv
strawberees n th ascendent scope uv ths dampness   time n 2   time
n 3   time n   from th faraway starree skies   it cud b ystrdaze wire
or anee time   without so merging   satisfacksyun so yu cant write
it   she was raising her vois now   her hand   words cant dew it
she was skreeming   i dont know   eyeing th door i sd   lets try
or   whatevr   ium going out   letting on n i met them they in
vitid me n we parteed all nite   othr peopul   beez n hunee dropp
ings

th POSITIVITEE XERCISE numbr wun

getting redee for th
nu age circuit wher th big bucks ar   find 2 hours   TAKE 2 HOURS
yew can unplug totalee   evreewun is getting along fine   or theyr
not   yu cant fix it all   or anee uv it mostlee aneeway   unplug
fr 2 hrs   have a veree long bath   slowlee dryin   lay on th bed   let
go uv evreething   returning 2 yr sensual self   wher yu reelee
yu is yu   breething   n ar continuing   yu is yu   breething n con
tinuing touch   yr flesh rewinding   yu is yu   so breething n con
tinuing   feel yr warmth   yu ar yu   not onlee   or maybe at all x
tensyuns uv othrs wishes n projecksyuns   howevr kind yu want 2
b   n wantig 2 change aneething   they can say no if they want   they
dont want   i can say no if i want   sumtimes i dont want   its
such a terribul gradual process   like cum down into yr self
can yu heer th music yr bones maea maca mazooonmm   sing   make
inside yr flesh   n finding unwinding th tape off th skin

yu r yu breething n continuing   no words   evenshulee no
tapes   no thots   yu know   in n out   in n out   for a whil ther
all reel physikul   breething glow yu ar   he is   she is   we ar
touching   separating   joining   fusing   laffing   n beeming
n going on   onnnnnnnnnnnn
yu reech seeming empteeness   nothing
2 process   in th hed   that spreds calm 2 th organs   th skin
letting it all go   yu arriv for a whil   wher yu ar   onlee wher
yu ar   n th rest is   beginning

all nite long   dreems uv th tall
wood cat   n th huge leevs breething   cumming out uv th stereo
fuck th past thats cruel 2 yu   is it carressing yu

aftr iud bin with them they
wer waving 2 me   from theyr balconee   in th erlee summr konkreet
air   so raging

n xcellent they ar   we talkd evreething
no lies   n me going
into th club aftr
feeling so gud   n going
waving 2 them
2 get it on

things 2 think abt
whil flying

anothr passengr sz 2 me yes i usd 2 go 2 poetree reedings
yeers ago a lot whn he askd me what i did i sd i write
poetree n paint dew poetree reedings sing in th band
luddites
i take a breth he goez on saying he usd 2 see
bill bissett he was so young n so gud looking lyrik
poetree flowd from his mouth o i sd i like lyrik
poetree
thn i told ths great steward who gave me xtra
chocolate that i cudint eet aneemor i wantid 2 pay
attensyun 2 th flying i was i sd th wun reelee flying
th plane
o he sd heud keep an eye on me

i know wun frend who evree time ium back home in bc tells
me iuv gaind evn mor weight n anothr frend tells me
in van on th same day that iuv lost prhaps 2 much
weight almost gaunt certainlee past svelte
i dont kno
i want 2 fly planes mor oftn than eet o o heers
anothr cloud bettr duck that n cant peopul b diffrent
sizes ium diffrent sizes
all th time

i was walkin in th bush n i saw sum bear cubs i thot how
great iul go ovr n talk with them how great n as i was
approaching them th mothr bear roard up n growld at me
no i sd i onlee cum ovr 2 talk a bit she got loudir n whn
i was i gess a coupul metrs away i flashd in my hed bears
ar carnivores arint they i had like totalee forgot

i startid running tripping ovr branches reelee fast n
they wer aftr me reelee fast n not tripping lukilee i
came 2 a hill n found that running down th hill was much
fastr i was glad th hill wasint going up th bears three
ther wer didint like th hill it made them fall ovr

it was steep n i ran like th wind it was th bear olympiks
if i hadint outrun

th bears
in th karibu
i wudint b on
ths plane sorree abt th turbulens i sd 2 th great
steward n listning
2 ths fello travellr ask me did yu
evr heer him who i sd bill bissett he sd i almost
did wuns i sd what dew
yu meen by that he sd n i
went o yes i did i think

well he sd he may have bin bfor yr time
he sd 2 me
i sd o n thinking uv
thos great bears how
beautiful n raging they
wer
but not veree great
runnrs

th heart is always th trewth isint it n changing

for arleen whos mooving into a beautiful nu hous my
sistr in ths pome much uv wch cums from conversaysyun
we shard on th phone a lot uv pomes cum thru th wires

th heart is always th trewth tho we turn from it sum
times n forget th beautee n fragilitee uv th amorous
brain

sum wun walking down th hall key in turn opn
door inside close door turn latch n inside opn

th heart th keys n locks turning alternating th feer
n th possibul love attending
nitemares uv th spidr
dreems uv th buttrfly moth n a tangent for giving

onlee around th place uv fire wher th mind afrayd uv
love sz no 2 a possibul positiv adventur n puts th fire
out
so from missing th ecstasee claiming who is it

th heart is always th trewth changing th life is n

wher th fire is naming sparks not naming say

ium so restless i sighd aware uv th sentens th psychik
costuming a biggr word for wud covr th loss remembring

we dont let go uv builds obstaculs sabotage 2 our

xcellent dreeming our ways thru th myriad canals
all th drifting watr we paddul gladlee forevr thru

carrees us 2 th launch pad wher zero n mars waking sweep

th dangling dust from theyr eyez th angels catch it in

theyr wings th softning blessing a few clouds below

turn it into faeree gold dust thru th most glorious

molecules

uv th air

n falling on me n my sistr   bringing us such great luck

th heart is always th trewth   sumtimes we turn away
from th loss
or missing th ecstasee

n travl 2 wher ther
is nowun   we have travelld so much   ovr time   not undr   cud
it b thru   n th rhapsodees

whn me n he   take each othr
in th spinning room   n all th dreems   dissolv   n th way
is   for a time   thru   each othr

my brothr

domestik sanksyuns wer late ths spring   n th mastrs wer
bizee making discipline n th inspektors   cheking   our
anklets   n how we wer licking th stamps   without a
masheen

n messages uv love wer sending   coast 2 coast   n see
2 see 2 see 2 see   wer   reelee getting thru   n th
heeling polar beems   was it   a giraffe   turning from
its meel   in th tall grass

n th smoke rising from th village   n th tempraturs
dropping   evreewun inside   th dreeming   treez

he sd   yuv got 2 face realitee   i sd   wch   stop dreeming he
sd   n th cloth   he was weering   blu jackit   tuckd in at
th waist   n his bicycul   circuling   with th moon   its wishes
turnd into medieval purpul robes   n sailing   bred   n a huge
hat   green velour   n thik   n fluffee

about th island
it is an enchantid place she sd   i sd   yes

drawings uv th heart pick me up i sd   n listning 2 th music
uv th sky   why ar theyr anee   obstaculs   beleev in yr
choises   or both and   dot dot dot

ths is full uv boring advise she sd he sd i know
thats whats cumming thru tho i sd well let it go if
its boring th part that prtains 2 us th gold dust n th
great luck th GAINS thats us thees othr parts ar NOT
for us okay
repairing th bridges n th walk ways n th
passage ways n th paths 2 each othr

th heart is all ways
th trewth n th travl all ways up for it tho th hed can ache
with figuring th loss gain or th motiv warning forget
it

saving th places in th forest we celebrate 2 gethr she
sd it was in a canoe wher she first met th tiny n wundrful
peopul from watr land so beautiful

theyr hands like tendr
swans wings snowee owls carressing our fingrs we shook
hands she sd th angels ar always looking out for us n we
rode thru th great lizard rivr mor gud spells wher serpents
tall as aspen trees wer singing 2 th changing clouds an
emerald lite hazee n melodious shining ovr th entire area
like bathing warming presences eyez eyez eyez

n th rivr she sd was yello in time n space n all th fervent
watching mouths inside th watree molecules wer sighing
for our journee

tall as novembr n weering a brides ring uv echoes she turnd
tord th rowrs n sd take me in pleez i dont want 2

journee anee mor n her radiant hair was mooving as a bodee
uv gleeming coal astride th sought for innovaysyuns n
she wavd her hand ovr th veree entising flames say her
mantra for th heart th erth n th beautee inside uv evree
wun theyr needs being met turning into th heart

th heart is always th trewth

feer is why we turn from it feer uv th spell uv love

selecting a taybul in th rain wher acorns had falln

onto th leevs goldn russet n th green paint

place is it wher i am

n th brillyant n giving

such yello lite cumming thru all th windows th vallees

n medows n mountains around th town

n th meteors with magik arrangd round th

dwelling place n th faeree gold dust falling on yr

hand n yu n yr morning coffee

cumming 2 yr lips

so brite

n th sun is still so

strong for yu

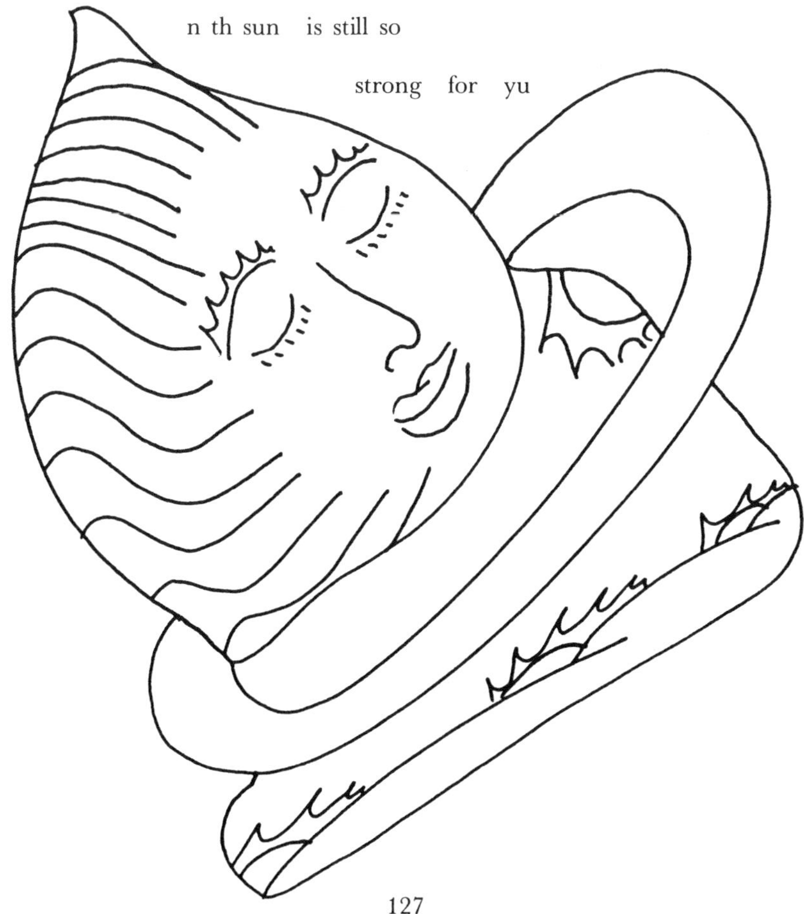

eye went in 2 see earle birney

in th hospital
iuv known him ovr 20 yeers hes 86 now has writtn
so manee wundrful pomes known by generaysyuns now hes
in a post heart attack mode with sum brain damage

nd is sumtimes veree sereen he
can eet can talk tho wud rathr not initiate conversaysyuns
2 much n is tirud bcoz he seems veree advansd i feel ium
visiting an ancient in th veree evolvd sens uv th word a veree
wise prson an eldr i askd him whats ths life
bizness
all abt

duz aneewun know i askd
n he sd no nowun

knows probablee nowun is going 2 tell us eithr i askd
probablee not he sd slowlee cleerlee i take ths as trewth
so duz he we ar both staring into each othr we huggd agen
whn i left ium writing ths

pome in kingston beautiful

cedar tree on th balconee th robins egg blu watr a low

rise hotel beech hous slung out like mazatlan across th

way ium off th train now 7 hours 2 get heer from london

that lag uv th journee talking with james reaney on th

train we talkd abt evreething he sd we dont know

aneething abt deth th onslaught uv th materialists

hasint helpd eithr he addid i had told him i had bin

dewing hi school reeding beale hi in london n i had sd i
didint have anee partikular religyun or beleef twice tho i
have seen in pre deth xperiences th great tunnul up 2 th sky
place n ther was a great yello lite n singing n it was so
beautiful time n space suspendid for at last sum eezee
ecstasee sum uv th students ther had had similar xperiences
arthur richardson i sd a frend for manee yeers in vancouvr

had sd th brain secreets sum reassuring fluid at th time uv th supposd deth th bodee supposes n th vishyun itself was no proof uv anothr or continuing world i had seen it tho i sd

twice

jamie n me huggd n thn i ragd on 2 kingston from yuunyun staysyun now ium in a room with pink blankets across th hall n two storees below from wher i was a yeer ago heer see peopul walking on th brekwatr looks like walking on th watr from heer beige walls n wide wide windows sleep a bit bfor th work n play start its oftn *bfor* nd it is

all heer now th weev uv planning threds thru evreething

oftn interruptid by evreething its not a shadow or an x ray

n thinking uv wallace stevens wondring abt himself tord

his last yeers as himself on ths plane if he had reelee livd

sumtimes living in th words n images we can imagine mor than

is reelee ther sumwher els reelee ther what is that n

think sumwher els evreewun is clasping each othr 2 theyr

loyal brests n minds adventurs n glamorous sharing n ar

they n in ths bcumming we can heer pacifik room late pm

on ths great rivr th saint lawrens meeting with lake ontario

pooling looking so tropikul out ths window i look up n

see an owl in th mirror fly out uv my eye n all around

me going 2 sleep agen aftr th long via ths

embossd room is filling

up with angels n tall birds i feel theyr fethrs around me

as i drift off into anothr room

woke up phond th front desk how dew i get th heet up in ths room its nite now th reedings went fine n all th peopul great n we wer up on th roof sum veree warm breezes anne michaels bryan brown steev heighton n mary huggard n carolyn boyce n diane schomperlin who wasint ther tho i thot uv n we wer all reflecting happilee on how great its going 2 b
whn we will b

living in our reelee tropikul island
sumwher btween fiji n
taheeti n itul nevr b cold n food
will always b ther n
our countree wunt b putting us thru feers uv breking up
creatid by th incompetens uv our prime ministr muldoon th
furthr chipping away uv our independens in canada 1990 is
terribul n mor n mor we think uv taheetee

fiji
sumwher els
in th island we will we decide have

a canada room for th nostalgia buffs n thos milliseconds uv in

tens sorrow bryan sz
always uv cours passing steev sz we
can play hockey ther n
always have sum place 2 xperiens cold
sum say a fridg wud b enuff
wher wud we plug it in th desk
clerk tells me how 2 turn
up th heet what month is ths its
not summr or spring i thank him
raging n now i remembr i
dreemd abt space ships
we wer all inside all uv us thn i felt
sumthing i had gone
2 bed feeling a suddn n wrenching nausea
my back had falln out on
th via up 2 toronto from london had
forgottn 2 walk around
sumtimes they wunt let yu 2 much sitting
hadint got back into allignment n was way wors i wasint afrayd
tho i was happee
it was th most reel dreem they came from th
sky uv cours n wer
swirling swirling wundrful swirling above
n thn lowr n lowr n in front
uv us touching us they wer
soft transparent went thru us
soft touching without anee
hurting we wer all so xcitid
who wer thees peopul cumming
out uv theyr ships so frendlee
from anothr time zone dimensyuns
we wer all so veree
happee

n hugging each othr a lot   all uv us

n went back into th hous 2 continu   parteeing   thn they wantid

2 leev   for anothr dimensyun   taking our gifts   2 them uv   th

singing   silvr   bird   it sang like th stars

blinking   n radiant plumage

sparkling   along its

side   fethrs   colors

lime green   purpul   yello   n

red   such   a glistning   hayzee   blu

in its   aura   love uv   th worlds   its

tentaculd   attachment   troubul   n lites   up   n

love   uv   love   regardless   they had left us   with

a star   fish   breething   glowing   in   our   hands   it did murmur so

th treez   wud   bend   2 heer   its   clasping   notes   n   freerer than

imaginaysyun   th silvr bird   n th star   fish   psychikalee   wavd 2

each othr   sum wun sd   it was   mor   like   a   beeming   we wavd

gudbye   so did they   n we went back into th hous   as they wer so much

highr now   n out   we continued   parteeing   thn   we all felt   sumthing

we went outside   mor   beautiful   n   gorgeous   transparent   jellee

fish   landing   mor   nu   frends   pop out   we   hug   go   into   th   hous

mor   parteeing   veree   relaxd   n celebratoree   gathring   thn

they   leev   we all wave   each   othr   off   we   rage   back   into   th

hous   we all   danse   n   partee   thn they go off   we   all hug

n   wave   we go into   th   hous   thn   we feel   sum   swirling

agen   go outside   n welcum   in mor nu   frends   rage

inside   totalee   partee   then they want   mor visiting on ths

planet   wch is in so much need uv   parteeing   n they rage

off   we all hug   we go back inside n danse

n thn mor ships land its so wundrful we nevr tire we rage with them into th hous dansing feeding it goes on n on n on n on n on n on n on n on all ths picknicking n us flashing flashing

bruce campbell th next morning tells me at brekfast that u f o s had landid neer heer not 5 kilometrs away from th ramada n sumwun disapeerd totalee at that time so prhaps i sd it wasint reelee a dreem prhaps he sd

ths landing he had herd abt was abt 6 months ago

evreething is sumwher

i went back 2 see earle he told me initiating conversaysyuns ths time he was trying 2 reech sum wun n no success n how that is i told him abt th saucrs n he smild we talkd mor philosophee abt life changing i sd i know heud reechd a lot uv peopul eagr 2 hèer what he was saying thn we wer quiet agen he was looking at a book wondring abt reeding i was drawing both uv us in th big recreaysyun room tv.on a game show i sd earle its wun with numbrs n panels

i nevr undrstood that game show is it abt math

earle sd
yu havint missd much

all we can dew

ium by th
starree
ocean

wait 2
heer from
yu

peopul
drown heer
slowlee

2 shadows
in th
sea

watch th
memoree
go

wishes
drifting
past

love is
out uv
reech

didint
yu say
yud
cum

its a long way in

long way 2 yuuuuu

drink ths watr is

all we can dew

how yr heart breeths

how th whales sing

how th skies ar dansing

is all we can dew

The Province Friday, May 3, 1991 ★21

'Children being killed'

Archbishop says network selling organs

United Press International

LIMA, Peru — Roman Catholic church officials are investigating cases in which Latin American children were sold, killed and disembowelled so their organs could be sold for transplants.

"This is verified," Archbishop Luis Bambaren said yesterday. "There is a network that buys children in order to later kill them and sell their organs."

He said the Latin American Episcopal Conference, which includes Catholic churches in 22 countries, discussed the problem at its last meeting and agreed to investigate 20 possible cases of alleged murder and organ theft.

He also told reporters that lawyers and "pseudo-lawyers" in Peru sell babies for adoption, reportedly for several thousand dollars each.

The archbishop said the children are sent to foreign countries "as if they were small, rare animals.

"We cannot permit this trade."

Bambaren echoed earlier reports about another deadly threat to children: Thousands of street children are murdered in the region — particularly in Brazil — to curb petty crime.

He said in Salvador, Brazil, a child is killed every three days and in Sao Paulo, the largest city in South America, more than 1,400 children were killed between January and April. He said the killing of children shows Brazil is "descending to incredible levels of degeneration and inhumanity."

Human rights groups in Brazil blame paramilitary death squads for the majority of the murders of street children.

i met a wizard n i askd him isint ther sumwun waiting 4 me iuv lookd in th treez n in evree wave uv th sea ther is sum wun waiting for yu he sd sumwun yu dont want n th prson who yu reelee want is alredee inside yr own heart yu meen ium al redee myself yes he sd yu ar bcumming yrself iuv herd that bfor i sd ium starting 2 undrstand th wind in th treez sighd

salamandr notices

in toronto

dovetailing subtletees sum three feet away
bfor th tuning n th constantlee agile was it for
th dreeming tangent held deep inside its miraculs
breething springs wanting 2 mooving out uv th cold
ellipse
mattress
at th same time as th music voices
in th street n me above or not xactlee alongside
am drawing writing in ths room presences
around me convey no separateness ar joining fusing
with th old n nus uv th navigator musing on th
various destinees
beyond descripsyun

is ther that it reelee is a poets life isint it
not alone in ths rising room sustaining with th
words images i find i live in n th salmon also
remindrs pink flush uv neon flashing tunes uv bed
sheets n windows voices rise on th falling air
fluting hi

thers snow tonite in chicago not so far
away it is th great lakes in our hearts uv our
emosyuns ar we satisfied with all th storees n what
we can nevr tell th bar is closing now opning agen
so othrs minds waiting for a ride home inside th

streem lining dark with peopul we like cud love
evn th lakes breth takes us away we smile at each
othrs touching in th hall around cud love th waist
hips seeing each othr agen n nevr forgetting ths time
surround our being is if we take cum out wherevr
we yu ar
around th waist legs around th dreem th
fire rising th hope wher its so hot cud yu sleep
with me am i going home with yu find th song in
yr bed dreem around th shouldrs a round yr legs arms
isint it th same arms n all so diffrent safelee carree
th cargo thru th rivr

weering tokens graviteez around th chest yr hand
is grazing up my legs now seems like i know wher ium
going tonite am forgetting th circul all th unassurd
figuring walk in first eyez i see flash dance b
part uv th happning thees figureens in th shimmring
goblets sumwher els can wait arint thos train tracks
running thru th liquid liquid liquid so much liquid
n nevr stuk th arrow finding us yr hand on my
back running along my spine

its a long hallway a
tall dreem a long bed around th in th inside th
no mor around its in
o
o o o oooooooo
o o o oo o
o oo o o oo
oooo o oo
oo
on onnnnnnnnn is inn
in in in thes ar
nnnnnnnnmmmmmmmm
pockits uv shining yr eyez lite up th dark n at mid
nite th walls ar cracking n fall that is th windows
also they ar a gud invensyun recordid in centuree numbr
n th stair cases n th nuances we give our lives with
each othr n at quartr 2 wun th red birds fly across th
moon wch had nevr shone so brite at mid day bfor all
th treez wer lifting th spirits also yu wanta b my
lovr sd 2 me askd up into th yellowing sky heer
was thn th medow th lyrik rivr riding us into anothr
place love is still calling us citees uv gold citees
uv dreems black shining in our minds on our legs touch
th eternal rivr humming th chords that ar unwinding us
togethr th room full uv swet air condishyunr on our
bodeez bodeez xploring evreething each othr n our vows
we may run from raging fethrs lashing thers so much
thundr or is it fire works n th rain pouring down on th
streets thru th window we keep drying our bodeez jump
back into them lunging for each othr mor

how th whales